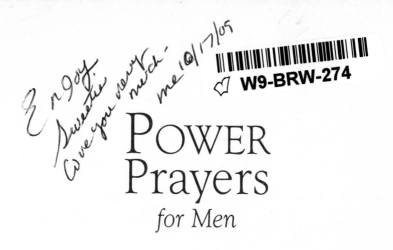

*Enjoy.
Sweetie
I love you very much
me 10/17/05*

POWER
Prayers
for Men

JOHN HUDSON TINER

BARBOUR
PUBLISHING

ISBN 978-1-59789-858-4

Published by Barbour Publishing, Inc., P.O. Box 719, Uhrichsville, Ohio 44683, www.barbourbooks.com

Our mission is to publish and distribute inspirational products offering exceptional value and biblical encouragement to the masses.

Member of the
Evangelical Christian
Publishers Association

Printed in the United States.

Dedicated to
Paul Conner Stephens

Contents

Introduction

The Power of Personal Prayer

*A*s a man, you face many special challenges in life—challenges that call for specific prayers. *Power Prayers for Men* is a vital tool and straightforward book on prayer, written from a man's point of view. Collected here are more than 350 short but powerful prayers that will help you face everyday issues with confidence. These prayers serve as a launchpad to a thoughtful, more dynamic prayer life. They will inspire and motivate you to seek God's power when you face difficult decisions.

Twenty-one chapters address topics of particular interest to men, such as responsibilities, health, finances, family life, salvation, dreams, and goals. Each chapter begins with an introduction that briefly sets the topic in context. Bible verses illustrate each topic and provide the biblical basis for prayer. Following each introduction are seventeen short prayers to launch your own prayers. Unique to each chapter are four or five prayers, observations, or exhortations from the Bible on that topic, prayed or passed on to us by Jesus or heroes of the faith.

Prayer changes circumstances, and it can change us. Instead of tossing and turning at night while grappling with difficult choices, turn them over to God in prayer. Instead of worrying about your next decision, ask God to show the way. God is listening, and He wants to hear from His children. When Manasseh king of Judah was taken prisoner, he asked for help. "And when he prayed to him, the LORD was moved by his entreaty and listened to his plea; so he brought him back to Jerusalem and to his kingdom. Then Manasseh knew that the LORD is God" (2 Chronicles 33:13). God listens to our prayers just as he listened to Manasseh's.

Prayer is two-way communication that involves both talking to God and listening to His voice. Through prayer we express our love to God, thank Him for our blessings, admit our sins, and request His intervention in difficult circumstances. Often, the return conversation from God doesn't consist of actual spoken words. Instead, He brings insight through His Word, opens new opportunities in our lives, makes visible blessings we have already received, and fortifies our lives in ways beyond our imagination.

Communication with God is a simple act with immense ramifications. Like a lever that allows us to use a small effort to move a large load, prayer invites the power of God into our lives, strengthens our spirits, and cements our robust relationship with God. Through it we can encourage our families and have a positive impact on our local communities and beyond.

In its simplest form, prayer is talking with God as a friend. By sharing our hopes, dreams, and concerns, friends develop deeper and more meaningful relationships. In the same way, when we pray to God daily in an informal, conversational way, we develop a close relationship with Him.

We become like the people with whom we spend time. By walking and talking with God, we become more like Him. Prayer molds us into His image. When we invite Him to direct our lives, we benefit from His wisdom. Like Noah, we learn to walk at His side and follow His guidance (see Genesis 6:9).

How should you pray? Prayer is a great time to express praise to the Creator. Let Him know that although you speak to Him as a friend, you also recognize His power, knowledge, and greatness. "Great is our Lord and mighty in power; his understanding has no limit" (Psalm 147:5).

Confessing sins brings relief from them: "If we confess

our sins, he is faithful and just and will forgive us our sins and purify us from all unrighteousness" (1 John 1:9). Confession provides two other benefits, as well. By recognizing failings and stating them to God, you become more tolerant of others' flaws. As you recognize how easily transgressions multiply, you feel motivated to avoid situations in which sin flourishes. Jesus Himself, in His model prayer, asked the heavenly Father not to lead His people into temptation, but to deliver them from the evil one.

Survey your life, and you'll discover countless blessings. Have you been successful? It's because God has provided you with the opportunities, skills, and abilities. Has failure been dogging you? Thank God, because He has sustained you through the difficult times. He has been with you in ordinary, everyday situations and in times of crisis. Thank Him for being mindful of your needs, regardless of the circumstances. God will never leave you or forsake you (Hebrews 13:5).

As you address the deep concerns in your life, your heart will become earnest. As you request God's immense power to come to your aid, you'll find yourself sending heartfelt and fervent prayers heavenward. And God will answer. The Bible is filled with examples of God's promises being received through prayer. God's promises have abundantly blessed Christians throughout the ages. Prayers have brought solutions to life-threatening problems, given endurance during trials, and developed inspiration to live the Christian life.

God has blessings waiting. However, they are not automatically conferred. You must ask for them through prayer. Your prayers will unleash the blessing He is holding for you. Jesus says, "Ask and it will be given to you; seek and you will find; knock and the door will be opened to you" (Matthew 7:7).

Are all prayer requests granted? Answers to prayers may be granted, but it's possible to ignore them. Solomon, for instance, asked for wisdom and received it, but as he grew older he refused to apply his God-given wisdom to his personal life and failed to be what God desired of him. "Was it not because of marriages like these that Solomon king of Israel sinned?" (Nehemiah 13:26).

A loving God, in fact, cannot answer some prayers. God doesn't answer prayers that are against His very nature. This is why it's essential to know His will through Bible study. When you have God's Word as your standard, you understand when a prayer can be answered and when it cannot be answered in the way you seek. As you grow in spiritual wisdom and learn more about holy scripture, you'll understand that God cannot grant requests that violate His very commandments.

Ask for an event to transpire that would violate His good will, and you're asking improperly. Such a prayer will not and cannot be answered. Understand that when you pray, you're praying for the will of God to work in you. James warned, "When you ask, you do not receive, because you ask with wrong motives" (James 4:3).

One key to effective prayer is to study the scriptures. Prayer that brings results is based on God's Word. After being baptized by John, Jesus ventured alone into the desert. For forty days He prepared for His public ministry. After that time, He faced temptation from Satan. To each temptation, Jesus replied, "It is written . . ." (Read Matthew 4:1–11.)

Often prayers appear to be unanswered because of our limited understanding. God fulfills His plans in our lives and broadens our frail pleas in ways that allow His greater plans to be done. Peter, for instance, went up on a roof to pray. We don't know the nature of his prayer, but from his reaction to the vision that followed—which opened the Gospel to gentiles—the response was far greater than what he had sought (Acts 10:9–23).

As with Peter, the answer to our prayers can be far in excess of our limited appeals. The prayers in this book will help you understand how to seek God's rich blessings.

My Bible

The Power of a Precious Treasure

Some experts list Gutenberg's printing press as the most important invention of the past one thousand years. The very first book he published was the holy Bible, because this humble printer recognized its importance. Gutenberg gave Christians an unparalleled ability to study God's Word thoroughly for themselves. Because of his invention, scientists, religious scholars, and thoughtful individuals of the past five centuries have shared their ideas easily and quickly.

English-speaking Christians are especially blessed; more Bible translations and Bible study aids are available in our language than in any other. Bible dictionaries and other texts for studying scripture line shelf after shelf in bookstores and libraries. Dedicated teachers conduct Bible studies tailored to all levels of expertise. Tools are available to nearly everyone who wants to become well versed in scripture.

The Bible is a book to be read. Read about twenty-five verses a day, and you'll read through the entire Bible, both Old and New Testaments, in about three years. Reading thirty verses a day—about four minutes—will take you through the New Testament in well under a year.

The Bible is a book to be studied. After you've finished

reading the entire Bible, you can launch into an in-depth study of a particular topic, such as salvation, grace, love, or faith. Or you can dig deeper to learn why individuals mentioned in Hebrews 11 are considered heroes of faith. You can use a variety of translations, dictionaries, and other helpful books to understand difficult passages.

Should you tire of one study, the Bible has such a wealth of material that you can switch to something else, such as the parables of Jesus or His miracles. Or you can follow the life of Christ in order with passages from each of the Gospels. Many study Bibles offer suggestions for developing a strategy for learning more about God's Word.

The Bible is a book for everyone. It has the power to touch lives of people regardless of their education or economic level. Two thousand years ago, uneducated shepherds and farmers listened with interest as Jesus related His parables. Today, the lives of well-educated city dwellers are touched by the same stories. Thoughtful individuals are moved by Paul's emotional farewell to his friends at Ephesus, in which he quotes Jesus' statement, "It is more blessed to give than to receive" (Acts 20:16–38). Those who enjoy an action story have their imaginations captured by the exciting adventure of Paul's shipwreck on the way to Rome (Acts 27:13–44). The Bible is also a storehouse of poetry, songs, and proverbs.

The Bible addresses the constants found in our lives, regardless of education, economic status, or station in life— sin, pride, selfishness, and fear. You'll find no contemporary book as effective at addressing those issues as the Bible.

Diligence in Reading Scripture

*U*ntil I come, devote yourself to the public reading of Scripture, to preaching and to teaching. Do not neglect your gift, which was given you through a prophetic message when the body of elders laid their hands on you.

Be diligent in these matters; give yourself wholly to them, so that everyone may see your progress (1 Timothy 4:13–15).

Spiritual Training

*H*eavenly Father, fitness experts claim I am what I eat. Personal sports trainers say that exercise gives me a healthy body. Lord, I understand that spiritually I am what I read. For the right spiritual life, I must read, study, and feast on Your Word. To be strong spiritually, I also need to exercise what I've learned. I pray I will take full advantage of the spiritual training and strengthening provided by Your Word.

Educate

*L*ord, throughout my educational career, I read many text-books. Yet rarely did I find any reference to the Bible. Your Word deals with the most difficult subject of all—the human heart. An education that prepares me to face the world must include an understanding of where I came from, how I am to live, and where I am going. I will turn to the Bible as my spiritual textbook.

Entertain

*F*ather, I'm thankful the Bible is an interesting book. Children's eyes light up when it's time to listen to a Bible story at bedtime. They are captivated by the wonderful stories of Bible heroes. Even I am held in the grip of stirring events such as when Daniel spent the night in the lions' den. Thank You for not only telling Your truth, but also clothing it in the events that happened to real people as they strove to serve You.

Booster Shot

*L*ord, when I was younger, I had to get a booster shot for some childhood diseases. Today I realize Satan tries to infect me in a variety of ways. I must guard continually against sin taking control of my life. I need both the booster shot of deep study and the continuous application of reading Your Word to make my life what it should be. I will delve into the Bible daily.

David's Prayer about God's Word

The law of the LORD is perfect, reviving the soul. The statutes of the LORD are trustworthy, making wise the simple. The precepts of the LORD are right, giving joy to the heart. The commands of the LORD are radiant, giving light to the eyes. The fear of the LORD is pure, enduring forever. The ordinances of the LORD are sure and altogether righteous. They are more precious than gold, than much pure gold; they are sweeter than honey, than honey from the comb (Psalm 19:7–10).

Book of the Ages

Lord, I read my Bible and I see a work of immense power. It's a vast, awe-inspiring chronicle that sweeps across the ages. Reading the Bible submerges me into interesting stories so simple that children can understand them. It gives me scholarly content that keeps philosophers in deep discussions. Its educational value exceeds that of the best textbook. And infusing it all is the story of Your love. It guides me along life's road. Thank You for providing Your Word.

Desert Oasis

*H*eavenly Father, as I traveled through the southwestern desert, I noticed how many towns had developed around a source of water. The fields around the town were green with life. Water gave life to the desert and drew settlers. Lord, I know, too, that the living water of Your Word gives life to me. I want to absorb Your Word so I will be refreshed and ever growing in Your will.

Delighting in God's Word

*H*ow can a young man keep his way pure? By living according to your word. I seek you with all my heart; do not let me stray from your commands. I have hidden your word in my heart that I might not sin against you. Praise be to you, O LORD; teach me your decrees. . . . I delight in your decrees; I will not neglect your word (Psalm 119:9–12, 16).

Faithful Student

*L*ord, I can choose to have a Bible in unread, pristine condition but a life in shambles. Or I can have a used, frayed Bible but a life well ordered by You. Lord, the Bible is my constant companion. It lights the way for my present life, and it opens the gates of heaven to reveal my future. It guides my heart and my mind to the right way of thinking. I pray I will be a faithful student of Your Word.

Food for Thought

*F*ather, when I was a small child, the food I ate helped my body grow. Now that I'm an adult, food gives me energy and repairs damaged tissue. When I first became a Christian, I read the Bible to help me mature as a Christian. Now I'm a more developed Christian, but I realize I need daily study of the Bible to revitalize and energize me. Lord, remind me to read the Bible to repair my soul from the damage of daily spiritual warfare.

Spiritual Growth

*F*ather, thank You for the simple Bible stories that captured my attention when I was young. I became involved with the dangers faced by Noah, Samson, David, and other heroes of the faith. Lord, I pray I will continue to let the Bible carry me in righteousness across the events in my life. I pray I will prepare for daily living and spiritual growth by studying Your Word.

Guiding Light

*Y*our word, O Lord, is eternal; it stands firm in the heavens. Your faithfulness continues through all generations; you established the earth, and it endures. Your laws endure to this day, for all things serve you. If your law had not been my delight, I would have perished in my affliction. Your word is a lamp to my feet and a light for my path (Psalm 119:89–92, 105).

Pillar of Truth

*L*ord, I'm in a world of swift changes. Nothing is permanent. Well-made items quickly become obsolete. Solid brick-and-mortar buildings deteriorate. Long-held social principles are called into question. But I'm refreshed when I turn to my Bible and renew myself with Your unchanging Word. Your Word is an everlasting and comforting pillar of truth that supports me as I see age take its toll on everything else around me.

Intellect

*Y*es, Lord, the Bible does appeal to my emotions, but it also engages my intellect. I can immerse the full power of my mind in its study. Your Word is so rich that I'm unable to exhaust its full impact with a lifetime of study. Regardless of the depth of my understanding, a vast ocean of truth still awaits my study. I'm thankful, Lord, for the deeper aspects of Your Word.

My Salvation

The Power to Rescue My Soul

Salvation, as a general term, means "deliverance from destruction." The word comes from the same root as the word *salvage*, meaning "to save the cargo of a ship sunk by a storm at sea." As Christians, we view salvation as the rescuing of the soul from the shipwreck of sin.

Pride, selfishness, and a self-righteous attitude can lead us into a sin-filled lifestyle. If we walk our self-directed course, we separate ourselves from God. We become so far from Him that we lose sight of Him. Problems arise that are beyond our ability to cope—sickness, grief, injustice, destructive dependencies, or emotional turmoil. If we are wise and recognize that we have lost our way, we call for rescue. God alone can rescue us, but we have separated ourselves from His holiness.

Sin is separation from God. We can't continue on the wrong path and draw closer to God. To draw near to Him, we must repent, make changes, and choose the right path. Salvation restores our walk with God when we put our faith in Him.

Salvation is a matter of faith. The strength of faith comes from the one in whom I put my faith. A strong faith misdirected to an unworthy target such as a religious leader, a government program, or my own ability has no saving power. On the other hand, as Jesus explains in Luke 17:6, faith as small as a mustard seed is powerful, provided it is faith in

God. I may on occasion have weak faith and at other times strong faith, but the power of salvation is not altered, because my faith is in the unchanging power of God.

God readily and freely gives salvation. However, we all recognize that God's underlying design of the universe includes the built-in requirement that the books must balance. Scientists, for instance, speak of the law of conservation of energy. If energy is used in one place, it must come from some other place. Our own daily observation shows that nothing is truly free. A free meal requires that someone else pay for it. The free gift of salvation and forgiveness of sins must come from another source. That source is Jesus Christ.

Sins can be forgiven only if a sacrifice is made for those sins. God sent His Son, Jesus Christ, to die on the cross and provide for our salvation. "For God so loved the world, that he gave his only begotten Son, that whosoever believeth in him should not perish, but have everlasting life" (John 3:16 KJV).

Because I have accepted salvation, I will emulate the life of Jesus. I will pray, read scripture, follow Jesus' example in baptism, join in fellowship with other believers, and share my joys and sorrows with them. I will strive to serve Jesus in every aspect of my life. But as I follow Jesus, I must remain humble and not think that I can justify my own salvation.

May Christ Dwell in Your Hearts

*I*n him and through faith in him we may approach God with freedom and confidence. I ask you, therefore, not to be discouraged because of my sufferings for you, which are your glory.

For this reason I kneel before the Father, from whom his whole family in heaven and on earth derives its name. I pray that out of his glorious riches he may strengthen you with power through his Spirit in your inner being, so that Christ may dwell in your hearts through faith (Ephesians 3:12–17).

Salvation Embraced

*H*eavenly Father, I have made the decision to be born again. I have embraced Your salvation and turned my life over to You. My desire is to grow in knowledge of Your will. I want to reform my life to reflect Your love. I will face daily tests, but I know You won't allow Satan to overwhelm me. Please guide me to bring the good news of Your salvation to others.

Walking with the Lord

*F*ather God, my goal is to walk with You. But in this world, I can become careless like a small child in a crowded and busy place. I become distracted and stray from You. Kindly and gently call me back to Your side. I'm privileged to be a child of the King. As Your son, I know You expect me to grow and become more like You. As I grow, I pray that I will willingly take on a greater role in bringing others into Your kingdom.

Free Indeed

*L*ord, when I travel, I see many hotels that claim to offer a free breakfast, but I view such statements with disbelief. I know the cost of the meal is part of the room price. I'm skeptical that anything can be entirely free. I understand that Your grace is free to me because it came at the price of Your Son. When I accept my salvation as a free gift, it removes self-righteous pride that I have done anything. My salvation becomes an even more precious gift.

Solomon's Dedication of the Temple

*F*orgive your people, who have sinned against you.

"Now, my God, may your eyes be open and your ears attentive to the prayers offered in this place.

"Now arise, O LORD God, and come to your resting place, you and the ark of your might. May your priests, O LORD God, be clothed with salvation, may your saints rejoice in your goodness. O LORD God, do not reject your anointed one. Remember the great love promised to David your servant" (2 Chronicles 6:39–42).

Faithful Service

*F*ather, when I first became a Christian, I feared You would ignore my prayers when I failed You. I based this belief upon my own human weakness—when others disappointed me, I would sometimes become angry and turn my back on them. But as I grew in understanding, I learned that You heard me even when I disappointed You. Your love renewed my determination to serve You more faithfully.

Strengthened Prayer

*W*hen, through prayer, I put myself in harmony with You, Jesus, my life becomes more vital. Strengthen my prayer life so my love, faith, and trust in You continue to grow. When I see my prayers answered, I'm encouraged to study Your Word and share Your saving grace with others. Open my eyes so I recognize the many different ways You answer my prayers.

Cleanse Me of Conceit

*L*ord God, may I recognize every good thing as a gift from You. Yes, I have succeeded because of my skill, ability, and knowledge. Now I realize that You have given me those things. At other times, unexpected opportunities opened to me. Now I know You smoothed the way. I will guard from self-sufficiency and pride in my accomplishments. I will fill my heart with a cheerful love for You. Cleanse me of conceit and replace it with humility.

Sin in the Camp

*T*hen Joshua tore his clothes and fell facedown to the ground before the ark of the LORD. . . . "O Lord, what can I say, now that Israel has been routed by its enemies? . . ."

The LORD said to Joshua, "Stand up! What are you doing down on your face? Israel has sinned; they have violated my covenant, which I commanded them to keep. . . . That is why the Israelites cannot stand against their enemies; they turn their backs and run because they have been made liable to destruction. I will not be with you anymore unless you destroy whatever among you is devoted to destruction.

"Go, consecrate the people. . . ."

Then the LORD said to Joshua, "Do not be afraid; do not be discouraged. Take the whole army with you, and go up and attack Ai. For I have delivered into your hands the king of Ai, his people, his city and his land" (Joshua 7:6, 8, 10–13; 8:1).

Ensnared

*L*ord, I've watched wildlife experts net a wild animal. Once the net falls, the more the animal struggles, the more it is ensnared. Finally, it becomes still with exhaustion. It can't free itself. Sin is like a net, and I can't disentangle myself from it alone. May I never become so independent that I reject the assistance of other Christians to free me from the snares of sin.

Sea of Forgiveness

*L*ord, I see all sorts of discarded items in lakes that have been drained. Covered in slime, they are even more disgusting than when tossed away. The evil one wants me to dredge up those sins You have forgiven and forgotten. He wants me to live in the past. Lord, point me instead to the future. With You, I'm free to try again without the baggage of past failures holding me down.

Stronger Christian

*F*ather, I wish to be a stronger Christian. Mold my life to be more like that of Jesus. Weaken my coveting of earthly things. Replace it with a burning desire for heaven. Give me the courage to rely on You always. When troubles come upon me, let them never weaken the good Christian qualities I've developed. Help me reach out to others, speaking of You and of heaven in my conversations with them.

Too Much Self

*L*ord, I have prayed for deliverance from the evil one and from those who would do me harm. I have asked for deliverance from destructive dependencies. But still I fail. Lord, deliver me from self-indulgence. Let me put away selfishness and therefore improve my relationship with You and other Christians. When I fail, remind me to replace too much self with more of You.

Speak with Boldness

*T*hey did what your power and will had decided beforehand should happen. Now, Lord, consider their threats and enable your servants to speak your word with great boldness. Stretch out your hand to heal and perform miraculous signs and wonders through the name of your holy servant Jesus.

After they prayed, the place where they were meeting was shaken. And they were all filled with the Holy Spirit and spoke the word of God boldly (Acts 4:28–31).

Holy Spirit

*L*ord, when Jesus left His disciples, He assured them that the Holy Spirit would help and comfort them. I, too, need the power of the Holy Spirit to guide me. My desire is to be fervent in prayer and in study of Your Word. I call upon the Holy Spirit to guide me in developing my knowledge and understanding of Your will. I open my heart to the Holy Spirit to lead me into a just and holy life.

Love, Grace, Comfort

*F*ather, each day I'm thankful for the full blessings of Your love and for the grace of my Savior, Jesus Christ. I'm also grateful for the guidance and comfort of the Holy Spirit. I may differ with other Christians in matters of opinion, but we remain fast in fellowship with one another, provided we listen to the Holy Spirit. Thank You that Your Holy Spirit continuously guides us in understanding Your love and the saving power of Jesus.

My Responsibilities

The Power of Respect

As a new Christian, I went through several stages as I searched for guidance in understanding my responsibilities. I certainly received a lot of advice from a variety of sources. Some emphasized what I must believe. Others emphasized what I must do. Frankly, I received conflicting advice that loaded me down with commitments that exceeded my ability. I became confused and disheartened. Other Christians confided in me that they faced the same challenge in their attempts to clarify their responsibilities.

I realized that I needed to read the Bible, listen to teachers, pray, and fast. In my reading, I discovered that on several occasions, people asked Jesus what God required of them. In one case, the person asking the question gave the answer: Love God and love your neighbor as yourself (Luke 10:25–28). "And who is my neighbor?" he asked. In response Jesus related the parable of the Samaritan who aided an injured man on the road to Jericho. At that time, Samaritans were members of a hated and despised race. Yet this Samaritan, according to Jesus, became a neighbor to the man who fell among thieves.

Some Christians use the acronym JOY—Jesus, others, yourself—to summarize the idea expressed by the two great commandments. Think first of Jesus, then of others, and finally of yourself. Always putting others first was a roadblock to me as a new Christian. Over time, I realized that by repeatedly neglecting my own needs in favor of others' needs, I was improperly devaluing myself. Jesus said, "In everything, do to others what you would have them do to you" (Matthew 7:12). His statement reveals that we are to understand our own self-worth because it is a measure of how to treat others.

In my case, the verse that helped me the most is found in the Old Testament. The prophet Micah writes, "He has showed you, O man, what is good. And what does the LORD require of you? To act justly and to love mercy and to walk humbly with your God" (Micah 6:8).

As Christians, we seek justice. We uphold what is just and insist upon fair dealing for everyone. We recognize each person as a creation of God and treat each person with respect. We intervene for those who can't speak for themselves.

As Christians, we love mercy. When justice has run its course, we then administer mercy. We are compassionate and sympathetic. We forgive because we understand that we are often in need of forgiveness.

As Christians, we walk humbly with God. As we become more acquainted with God's Word, we understand that our outward actions are merely signs of a deeper commitment to God. Our primary responsibility is to be someone who walks with God.

Ananias, "Go!"

*I*n Damascus there was a disciple named Ananias. The Lord called to him in a vision, "Ananias!"

"Yes, Lord," he answered.

The Lord told him, "Go to the house of Judas on Straight Street and ask for a man from Tarsus named Saul, for he is praying. . . ."

"Lord," Ananias answered, "I have heard many reports about this man and all the harm he has done to your saints in Jerusalem. . . ."

But the Lord said to Ananias, "Go! This man is my chosen instrument" (Acts 9:10–11, 13, 15).

Vital Message

*L*ord, I have the honor of representing You and telling others the good news of Your salvation. Thank You for giving me a simple salvation plan that I can understand and share. I want to bear the vital message that salvation is found only in Jesus. Fill me with joy and resolve in my quest to express Your love for a world in sin. Help me deliver the beauty and wonder of Your peace.

Sow, Water, Increase

*L*ord, when I read exploits of New Testament disciples and modern-day missionaries, I realize my efforts pale in comparison to theirs. I take comfort that I can bring Your love to others through my present position and daily activities. I can sow a seed here and there through open and honest concern for others. I can encourage spiritual growth by living my life so others see Christian principles at work. I pray I will look for opportunities to open others' hearts to accept salvation.

Personal Responsibility

*L*ord, give me a sense of personal responsibility for the lost. I pray I can overcome irrational concerns that keep me from doing those things I know I should do. Give me courage that dominates my fears. Teach me ways I can bless others. Strengthen my decision to lead others to You. May I progress from my home to my neighbors to my extended family. Almighty God, I surrender myself to Your service.

Jeremiah's Prayer about God's Wisdom

O great and powerful God, whose name is the LORD Almighty, great are your purposes and mighty are your deeds. Your eyes are open to all the ways of men; you reward everyone according to his conduct and as his deeds deserve. You performed miraculous signs and wonders in Egypt and have continued them to this day, both in Israel and among all mankind, and have gained the renown that is still yours" (Jeremiah 32:18–20).

Living Offering

*L*ord, I understand that pagan cultures demanded a human sacrifice during a time of crisis. They believed such a fearful action would gain the attention and favor of the false gods they worshipped. Lord, Your love for us is illustrated by the fact that instead of requiring our blood, You gave Your blood for us. Only the God of Christianity gave Himself for His people. Thank You, Lord. I will dedicate my life to You as a living offering so others will see the blessings that come from knowing You.

Nominal Christian

*L*ord, keep me from following the path of a nominal Christian. I may listen to sermons, pray, fast, read the Bible, and then feel satisfied with myself. Remind me that actions devoid of love are empty. May I never think that doing for You is more important than being with You. I often need to be reminded of this fact. Help me lend energy to my actions through my love for You.

Trust and Leadership

*G*uide me, Lord, when my responsibilities require me to be a leader. Acting alone, I will be unable to fulfill my mission. Help me accomplish my role by recruiting others. Give me the ability to motivate and inspire. Fill me with energy and enthusiasm that I can convey to others. To be successful, I know I must trust others. May I do this by first putting my trust in You.

God Is with Us

*G*od called to him [Moses] from within the bush, "Moses! Moses!"

And Moses said, "Here I am." . . .

[God said,] "So now, go. I am sending you to Pharaoh to bring my people the Israelites out of Egypt."

But Moses said to God, "Who am I, that I should go to Pharaoh and bring the Israelites out of Egypt?"

And God said, "I will be with you" (Exodus 3:4, 10–12).

Hero of Faith

*L*ord, I've seen individuals with innovative ideas become bitter after quarreling with their critics, while others retained their joyful nature even though their ideas were dismissed. I'm not surprised that those who remained upbeat were Christians. Their most important goal was to be true to their Christian faith. I pray I will always remember to put You first, and then whether I win or lose in other aspects of my life, I will be a hero of faith.

Persuasive Representative

*Y*ou have made the greatest difference in my life. I want to be a persuasive representative for You to my family and friends. Direct me in my speech so I can effectively convey to them how You can change their lives, too. May I grow in knowledge, wisdom, and character. Give me the confidence to talk to others and instill in them a desire to learn more about Your plan for their lives.

No Shortcut

*L*ord, when I drive, I often decide to try a shortcut. I imagine it will be better than the usual route. Often, my alternate choice turns out to be a narrow, twisting road with hidden entrances and unexpected stop signs. Lord, help me realize I can't direct my own steps when it comes to my Christian journey. You have gone before me and found the best way. By walking in Your footsteps, I will follow a superior route.

Many Hats of Leadership

*F*ather, I wear many hats of leadership—husband, father, and worker both at my job and at church. Each carries a different set of skills and different ways of applying them. I pray that in each I will happily accept the responsibility to serve as a leader. I must not renounce my obligation merely because the job appears too difficult. May I never doubt that You have given me the personal skills to fulfill my leadership roles successfully.

Moses' Request to Be Excused

*M*oses said to the LORD, "O Lord, I have never been eloquent, neither in the past nor since you have spoken to your servant. I am slow of speech and tongue."

The LORD said to him, "Who gave man his mouth? Who makes him deaf or mute? Who gives him sight or makes him blind? Is it not I, the LORD? Now go; I will help you speak and will teach you what to say."

But Moses said, "O Lord, please send someone else to do it" (Exodus 4:10–13).

Chosen to Serve

*F*ather, at an assembly of the church, I expect to be renewed, strengthened, and aligned with Your will. I understand that to reach those goals, I must assist others and accept those assignments for which I've been chosen to serve. Often, Lord, I can find excuses for avoiding my obligations. Help me understand that when I neglect these opportunities to serve, I'm also neglecting my spiritual growth.

Keeping Fit

*L*ord, because of my sedentary job, I must take the time to exercise to stay in shape. Unused muscles go slack. Only a good, well-directed exercise program will keep me healthy. I realize that if I don't work at it, my spiritual life will become weak, too. Should I become slack in reading Your Word, praying, and thinking upon spiritual truths, I will become spiritually feeble. Help me make time for spiritual strengthening.

The Power of Becoming One

Marriage is the legal union of a man and a woman as husband and wife. But clues to how newlyweds will relate to each other can be seen even before the wedding. A young woman who treats her father with love and respect is likely to treat her husband the same way. The way a young man treats his mother is a mirror of how he will behave toward his wife.

Marriage begins with optimism. The husband is certain his bride will stay the sweet woman he married, and a wife believes she can change the groom into the man she wants him to be. Both have unrealistic expectations, and both will be disappointed.

When my wife and I married, procrastination was one of my strong suits. I seldom put off until tomorrow what I could get out of doing altogether. I had a high threshold of inaction. She, on the other hand, had the motto "If it's not broken, work on it anyway to make it better." I thought we would influence each other to a happy medium.

I had unrealistic expectations about how she would change, and she had unrealistic expectations that she could change me for the better. We both saw problems in ourselves and in each other, and we both thought marriage would mitigate those problems. We were deeply mistaken.

The Bible says, "For this reason a man will leave his father and mother and be united to his wife, and they will become one flesh" (Genesis 2:24). Becoming one is a process of change. Neither husband nor wife is particularly happy about being the one to modify behavior. The goal, however, is not for me to become the man she wants or for her to become the woman I want, but for each of us to become the person God wants. The Bible says, "Has not the LORD made them one? In flesh and spirit they are his. And why one? Because he was seeking godly offspring. So guard yourself in your spirit, and do not break faith with the wife of your youth" (Malachi 2:15).

If a husband and wife stop working on their marriage, it comes to a halt. It must be rebuilt every day. Once husband and wife realize that all is not peachy keen, a time of reevaluation begins. The process is usually long on talking and short on listening, but true communication involves both hearing and being heard.

It's wise for communication to begin with positive aims. In your own marriage, you can begin with a review of what each of you liked in the other. What attractive qualities led you to marriage? Identifying those attributes and strengthening them will crowd out some unattractive traits.

As you grow closer to Christ, you grow closer to each other. Share your goals and ambitions, support each other, and pray for each other, and you'll build a marriage that will last a lifetime.

Noble Wife

A wife of noble character who can find? She is worth far more than rubies. Her husband has full confidence in her and lacks nothing of value. She brings him good, not harm, all the days of her life. . . . "Many women do noble things, but you surpass them all." Charm is deceptive, and beauty is fleeting; but a woman who fears the LORD is to be praised. Give her the reward she has earned, and let her works bring her praise at the city gate (Proverbs 31:10–12, 29–31).

Blessed Companion

*L*ord, as I count my blessings this morning, I begin with my wife. She has blessed me throughout the days in many ways. I've had medical problems, but she has been at my side to encourage me. When problems became greater than I could carry, she was there to share the load. When things seemed bleak, she reminded me that we were not alone, because You were with us. I will continue to give thanks to You for her.

Talking Out Loud

*L*ord, when I'm uncertain of what to do, I often find that I need to think out loud. Only by talking things out can I come to a full understanding of a problem. I'm thankful, Lord, that my wife is willing to listen to these rambling monologues. When she does speak, she often clarifies my thinking concerning the essential aspects of my problem. Even if she doesn't offer any suggestion, her very presence gives me confidence. Thank You, Lord, for her.

Too Much Baggage

*L*ord, when my wife and I return from a vacation, we take note of items we didn't use and replace them with ones more suitable for our travels. Lord, a marriage is a long journey that accumulates unnecessary baggage. As imperfect people, we have times of disagreement. I ask that we each identify and discard those painful memories that create mistrust and discord. May we restore our relationship with renewed love and respect for each other.

Royal Bride

*L*ord, Your Word describes Your loving consideration for the church as an example of how a husband should treat his wife. Nothing separates me from Your love. In the same way, neither should my wife be separated from my love. I pray I will learn more fully of Your love and emulate it in my conduct with my wife. May our love for each other be as enduring as Your love for us and for the church.

Love Is Strong

*P*lace me like a seal over your heart, like a seal on your arm; for love is as strong as death, its jealousy unyielding as the grave. It burns like blazing fire, like a mighty flame. Many waters cannot quench love; rivers cannot wash it away. If one were to give all the wealth of his house for love, it would be utterly scorned (Song of Songs 8:6–7).

Temporary Duty

*L*ord, keep me united with my wife and family when temporary duty takes me away from them. Although we speak on the telephone and send messages by e-mail, the personal communication of a face-to-face meeting is lost. Be with each of us. May our prayers rise up to You in one spirit. Protect me on my journey. No matter how far I am from them, may they still feel my loving presence.

Reflecting Grace

*B*lessed Savior, You have set marriage as an example of the union between You and Your church. I earnestly pray for Your blessing on our marriage. Grant to both of us a union full of mutual benefits and comforts. May we each have love and respect for each other. Help us reflect the same grace and kindness that You show to Your church. May we daily become more like You.

Diversity and Shared Interests

*L*ord, when my wife and I first married, our mutual interests were few. Yet our marriage thrived because we both took seriously the idea of commitment. We each continued our own leisure pursuits, but we found time for each other and developed shared interests. Lord, I pray that I will continue to be committed to my marriage and that my wife and I will remain dedicated to each other.

Fadeless Love

*L*ord, You love Your people and describe believers as Your spouse. As a husband, I pray I will model my feelings for my wife in the same way. Help me keep the special affection that I had for my wife when we were first married. May I be constant in my love. Make it possible for others to say, "He loved her with a bond that was exceeded only by Jesus' love for the church."

Be as One

*H*usbands, love your wives, just as Christ loved the church and gave himself up for her. . . . In this same way, husbands ought to love their wives as their own bodies. He who loves his wife loves himself. After all, no one ever hated his own body, but he feeds and cares for it. . . . "For this reason a man will leave his father and mother and be united to his wife, and the two will become one flesh" (Ephesians 5:25, 28–29, 31).

Respect and Communication

*L*ord, I'm determined to live a life worthy of my wife's respect, and I will respect her as a faithful partner. I will share with her my dreams, fears, and goals. By talking with her, I will show that I value her opinion. I will also give her my time and attention as she shares with me the events of her life. Keep alive between us an open line of communication so we will relate well to each other.

Plan B

*L*ord, on those mornings when I must get up at an early hour, I keep a battery-powered clock on hand to back up the electric alarm in case of a power failure. My wife says I always have a plan B. She, on the other hand, is flexible and capable of easily and quickly modifying a plan to make it work. Lord, I recognize our differences and rejoice in them. May we always take advantage of our individual talents to accomplish a unified purpose.

Subtle Dangers

*L*ord, I had to take an alternate route to work this morning. A bridge along my usual way was closed. Regular inspection showed that rust and crumbled concrete had made it unsafe. I realize I always need to be alert to subtle dangers that threaten my marriage. May I always be active in making certain my marriage is not in danger of slow decay. May my wife and I keep our marriage intact as we share mutual respect and love.

Prayer of Confidence

I call on you, O God, for you will answer me; give ear to me and hear my prayer. Show the wonder of your great love, you who save by your right hand those who take refuge in you from their foes. Keep me as the apple of your eye; hide me in the shadow of your wings from the wicked who assail me, from my mortal enemies who surround me (Psalm 17:6–9).

Great and Small

*L*ord, when time seems to be passing too slowly, I look at the two dots between the hour and minutes of my digital clock. If they blink on and off, I know the clock is running. Lord, I want to closely monitor all facets of my marriage, both great and small. No matter how brilliantly I may think I'm handling major tasks, the small ones are important, too. Give me the ability to keep all aspects of my marriage functioning smoothly, from the great to the small.

My Children

The Power of Positive Training

*T*he future of a family—and a nation—depends on how well children are nurtured, trained, and corrected. Though governments recognize the importance of education, public school curricula seldom include ethical and spiritual training. As a father, I'm responsible for restoring the balance to my children's development. I will influence them for a lifetime.

My children have no greater need than my attention. I must devote time to my little ones while I have them, because they will grow up soon and the opportunity will be lost.

My children need instruction. Teaching begins with my clearly telling them what I expect of them. I should strive to develop the ability to explain things well, using language my children can understand. Small children are literal-minded, so I need to remember that a positive instruction describing the action I want is more effective than a negative one that identifies the undesired action. "Write on paper" is better than "Don't write on the walls." The Sermon on the Mount (Matthew 5:3–7:29) is a remarkable teaching example because Jesus begins with a list of more than ten positive blessings.

My children need training. Training my children to form good habits means that I must lead and direct their growth. Encouragement improves performance, while criticism puts a damper on it. I will shout appreciation for good behavior but explain an error privately and with a gentle voice. Once my children are properly trained, it will be very difficult for them to go against that early training. "Train a child in the way he should go, and when he is old he will not turn from it" (Proverbs 22:6).

My children need discipline. I think of discipline as correction rather than punishment. Discipline is a positive concept—discipline makes a disciple, one who follows a leader.

My children need me to be engaged in their welfare. Children in a home with a loving father are far more likely to complete their education and find secure employment, and they are far less likely to appear before a judge. The dark side of teen years—drug abuse, sexual immorality, and suicide—is less likely to occur if I remain engaged as a father.

I will call in help when it's needed. A male relative, a scout leader, or a church youth leader can give insight into a problem I've failed to see. The Bible says, "Where no counsel is, the people fall: but in the multitude of counsellors there is safety" (Proverbs 11:14 KJV).

My children need to see me pray. A daily prayer with my children is a powerful example of the importance of communion with God and of their importance to me. I will pray for the guidance of God so my children will grow up with strong Christian personalities.

Promise Kept

*S*olomon said: "O LORD, God of Israel, there is no God like you in heaven or on earth—you who keep your covenant of love with your servants who continue wholeheartedly in your way. You have kept your promise to your servant David my father; with your mouth you have promised and with your hand you have fulfilled it—as it is today" (2 Chronicles 6:14–15).

My Central Duty

*L*ord, earlier in my life, I imagined that the central duty of the parent-children relationship fell upon the children. I thought children should scramble to conform to the whim of the parent. Now that I've become a parent, and as I learn more about You as a loving Father, I'm more fully aware of the accountability that falls upon a parent. Remind me that my central duty is not to exasperate my children but to bring them up in Your training and instruction.

Unto the Next Generation

*L*ord, a family friend planted fruit trees, although years would pass before anyone benefited from his action. I realize that it takes a special individual to plan for the next generation. Develop an obligation in me to pass on what I have received and add to it. Let me plant seeds in my children's hearts. May I nourish them so they grow into honest and upright citizens who reflect their Creator.

Children of Power

*H*eavenly Father, I pray my children will understand that they can make a difference through prayer. May they recognize Your power and what they can accomplish when they pray in Your will. May they pray daily so that they will grow in faith and become the Christian leaders this country needs. I ask You to anoint them with wisdom and give them strength and protection. My desire is that they choose to walk in Your will all of their days.

Reasoned Response

*L*ord, when a crisis occurs, we seldom take time to make a reasoned response. At work we train for the unexpected and develop remedial actions. Lord, give me the insight to see the challenges my children will face. Help me prepare them for the tests. When faced with temptation, may they recognize the evil and rely on a sound solution that we have worked out from Your Word.

Pursuing Righteousness

*F*ather, help me steer my children to pursue righteousness. Help me develop their courage, endurance, and good judgment. My desire is to establish in their hearts the right choices so they will follow them despite adversity. Help me encourage them to be gallant in upholding the values that reflect Your holiness. Let them understand that You're beside them so they can overcome their fears when pursuing a noble purpose.

Lord's Servant

*T*he angel said to her, "Do not be afraid, Mary, you have found favor with God. You will be with child and give birth to a son, and you are to give him the name Jesus. He will be great and will be called the Son of the Most High. The Lord God will give him the throne of his father David. . . ."

"I am the Lord's servant," Mary answered. "May it be to me as you have said" (Luke 1:30–32, 38).

Motivation and Expectation

*L*ord, as I matured from childhood, I passed through a period of disillusionment. I discovered my heroes weren't as valiant as I first believed. Help me encourage my children to emulate what is good and honest. But may they not become cynical when they find that their role models are less than perfect. Give me the wisdom to encourage them to have an optimistic outlook without unreasonable expectations of those they trust.

Earthly and Heavenly Fathers

*F*ather God, how my children perceive me, their earthly father, will influence how they view You, their heavenly Father. I pray I will be the proper example of You in their lives by showing affection, benevolence, and consideration. I know Your love is unchangeable and filled with power and wisdom. Bless me as I strive to develop the same unchangeable love for my family. Strengthen my resolve to illustrate Your devotion to those in my life.

Emulate and Escape

*L*ord, may I live in a way that is a credit to You. Although I pursue worthy goals as part of my Christian values, I know there will be times when I fail. Rather than concealing my shortcomings from my children, I want to be open and honest about my imperfections. I want them to see my positive examples and emulate the successes, but also learn from my failures so they escape the consequences of such wrong choices.

Hannah's Prayer for a Child

*S*he made a vow, saying, "O LORD Almighty, if you will only look upon your servant's misery and remember me, and not forget your servant but give her a son, then I will give him to the LORD for all the days of his life, and no razor will ever be used on his head" (1 Samuel 1:11).

Far-Flung Families

*L*ord, older parents tell me they find it difficult to keep in touch with their far-flung families and stay involved in their lives. I, too, am finding it increasingly difficult to spend time with my children. As they grow older, they become more involved in activities outside the home. I want to give them the freedom to mature, but I want to be knowledgeable about their lives and remain a valuable resource for their guidance, especially in spiritual matters.

Standards

*J*esus, I pray my children cling more firmly to Your teachings as a guide for their lives. As they mature, may they not steer their lives by the standards of society, which are skewed by expediency and materialism. I pray they observe the laws of their nation but develop the courage never to let those laws that contradict Your holy Word take precedent over Your precepts.

You Saw Suffering

*Y*ou saw the suffering of our forefathers in Egypt; you heard their cry at the Red Sea. . . . You divided the sea before them, so that they passed through it on dry ground, but you hurled their pursuers into the depths, like a stone into mighty waters. By day you led them with a pillar of cloud, and by night with a pillar of fire to give them light on the way they were to take (Nehemiah 9:9, 11–12).

Correct Perception

*F*ather, when I was a child, my friends and I had a variety of incorrect perceptions of You. We saw You as an angry judge or a harsh taskmaster or a distant sovereign unconcerned with our lives. Lord, now I understand that You aren't wrathful, unreasonable, callous, or aloof. Lord, help me reveal to my children the correct perception of You as a loving Father who is nearby and listens to their prayers.

Parenting

*L*ord, I can relate to my children in a variety of ways, including teacher, friend, and parent. When they were young, I was a teacher who trained them in all aspects of their development. Now that they are older, I listen as they talk out their problems and gently guide them to the best decisions. I pray I choose the role that is most appropriate to the situation. But may I never relinquish my parental duties as protector, mentor, and dispenser of necessary discipline.

My Home

The Power of a Spiritual Stronghold

*T*he home has an important role to play in Christian life. It's a physical and spiritual stronghold from which God sends out His people into the world. As fathers, we need to recognize some principles about the godly homes our heavenly Father encourages us to establish.

Home is a place of refuge. In addition to being a place to eat, sleep, and watch television, it's a safe haven, a place to seek protection from a harsh world. When we build our home lives as God intended, all members of a family look forward to coming home to a comforting welcome. Children find encouragement and support. Parents can relax, relieve tension, and reduce stress.

Home is a training ground for the next generation. A nation will prosper with Christian leaders, and often the next generation of them is trained in Christian homes. Training takes skill, dedication, and time. It requires us to avoid over-extending ourselves at work. Otherwise, we will come home totally exhausted and without the emotional reserve required to deal thoughtfully and pleasantly with our children.

Home is a place of balanced duties. For children, there is the admonition from Colossians 3:20, "Children, obey your parents in everything, for this pleases the Lord." Ephesians

6:4 gives balance by an instruction to fathers: "Fathers, do not exasperate your children; instead, bring them up in the training and instruction of the Lord." Ephesians 5:24 tells wives, "Now as the church submits to Christ, so also wives should submit to their husbands in everything." The next verse gives the balancing statement to husbands: "Husbands, love your wives, just as Christ loved the church and gave himself up for her."

As a father, I'm the anchor of the family. Of my many roles, the most important is to sacrifice as Jesus sacrificed for the church. Jesus gave His life for the church. I'm to give a portion of my life—my time—to ensure the spiritual survival of my household. I will give time to my children, but I can't neglect my wife. One day the children will be grown and leave home. If I haven't paid proper attention to my wife, we will feel an emptiness that will be difficult to bridge.

Home is a spiritual stronghold. In a world apathetic or even hostile to Christianity, my home is the last safe place for my family to fully express our religious beliefs. "Merry Christmas" may become "Happy Holidays" or even "Season's Greetings" in the secular world. But inside the home, all aspects of Christianity can be embraced. The home is where Christian principles are modeled by parents and emulated by children.

Home is to be built by God. The Bible says, "Unless the LORD builds the house, its builders labor in vain" (Psalm 127:1). A home is more than a residence. It's a place where each individual in a family reaches his or her full potential. This will happen provided husband, wife, and children choose to be in spiritual agreement with God and with one another.

Moses' Prayer after the Red Sea Crossing

The LORD is my strength and my song; he has become my salvation. He is my God, and I will praise him, my father's God, and I will exalt him. . . .

"In your unfailing love you will lead the people you have redeemed. In your strength you will guide them to your holy dwelling. . . .

"You will bring them in and plant them on the mountain of your inheritance—the place, O LORD, you made for your dwelling, the sanctuary, O Lord, your hands established" (Exodus 15:2, 13, 17).

Place of Refuge

Lord, I pray our home is a place of security, a place to come to be renewed and strengthened. May I teach my family to pray, and may I pray for them. May I teach them to be honest, and may I be honest with them. Help us support one another in unity and peace. In all aspects, help our home be a place of encouragement.

Home of the Soul

*F*ather, I'm determined to make a home that provides for my family and protects them. When we come together at the end of the day, I want to provide shelter, food, clothes, and a comfortable and secure place to rest. Lord, You have a home that provides all Your children's needs, too. Thank You for giving me the ability to provide for my family and to point them to a home not made with hands.

Private Personality

*H*eavenly Father, my job often requires me to exercise more patience than I normally possess. I must stifle irritations and restrain my natural inclinations. Lord, it's a great relief to come home and be myself. Help me keep the freedom at home from being an excuse to treat my family with less consideration than the strangers I meet at work. Instead, I ask that I act toward them with deference, honor, and thoughtfulness.

Thinking Ahead

*L*ord, I have a pilot friend who talks about thinking ahead of the plane. He says that to fly into a congested area, he must always be ready for his next two actions. Lord, being the head of a household also requires that I keep thinking about the future. Help me realize that I should not only do what is expected of me, but also anticipate what may happen next. Give me the ability to anticipate problems and overcome them while they are still of manageable size.

Moses' Prayer for God's People

I prayed to the LORD and said, "O Sovereign LORD, do not destroy your people, your own inheritance that you redeemed by your great power and brought out of Egypt with a mighty hand. Remember your servants Abraham, Isaac and Jacob. Overlook the stubbornness of this people, their wickedness and their sin. . . . They are your people, your inheritance that you brought out by your great power and your outstretched arm" (Deuteronomy 9:26–27, 29).

Boundaries

O Father, grant me the wisdom to see clearly the needs of my family. May we recognize those forces that would lead us away from the proper path. I ask for the skill to guide my family safely away from peril without putting unwarranted pressure on them, and I ask that they accept my leadership without resentment. Give us a home that encourages strength, dignity, and self-worth based on Christian values.

Home with Love

*L*ord, my home is attractive. It has a well-kept yard, a nice exterior, and good furnishings. But those things aren't what make it attractive. I come home to it because my loved ones are there. Should everyone be away but me, the empty house feels hollow. The residence is cold and lonely because those who saturate it with love aren't there. I pray my home will always be alive with the love of my family.

Late for Home

*F*ather, I've had to travel in my job. I feel as if my only connection with my family is the monthly mortgage payment on the house. I miss my wife and children. I'm concerned that I've put too much emphasis on making a good income. I'm seeking ways to have more time at home. Father, give me the opportunity to balance my home life with my career.

David's Prayer of Praise

*T*hen King David went in and sat before the LORD, and he said: "Who am I, O LORD God, and what is my family, that you have brought me this far? And as if this were not enough in your sight, O God, you have spoken about the future of the house of your servant. You have looked on me as though I were the most exalted of men, O LORD God" (1 Chronicles 17:16–17).

Happy Times

*M*erciful Father, I appreciate the rich blessings that fall upon me at home. Although not every day reaches perfection, those happy moments do arise when my wife, children, and I are aware of one another and appreciate one another. In that warm and loving atmosphere, we are drawn together in our special relationship. I pray we will pause to savor those moments. On a small scale we experience what heaven must be like.

Head of the House

*L*ord, according to the IRS, I am the head of my household. Certainly no one else wants that title. Occasionally, however, I feel woefully inadequate to be the leader of my wife and children. Show me how to accept my responsibilities. I pray my family will follow my direction by choice, out of love and respect. I ask that whenever I make a poor decision, You will rectify the outcome so none of those under my charge are harmed.

Pride and Delight

*F*ather, may I never point with pride at my house but rather with delight at those who live in it. May I never purchase a car to boost my ego but rather to transport me and my family to fulfill our purposes. May my motives for advancement at work be for the opportunity to strengthen my family in our service to You. I ask that my most prized possessions be not earthly ones, but the treasures being laid up in heaven.

A Life Worthy of the Lord

*F*or this reason, since the day we heard about you, we have not stopped praying for you and asking God to fill you with the knowledge of his will through all spiritual wisdom and understanding. And we pray this in order that you may live a life worthy of the Lord and may please him in every way: bearing fruit in every good work, growing in the knowledge of God (Colossians 1:9–10).

Newborn Eyes

*L*ord, the trusting face of a newborn baby can change a man and woman and cause them to rethink their lives. When I hold a newborn for the first time, with sudden awareness I see a greater world and the promise of the future. Lord, as I look at my child, may I see beyond the present to the world of the future. May I prepare a happy, spiritual home that points to the heavenly home You have prepared for us.

Anger Management

*F*ather God, I face countless opportunities to become angry, especially at home with a multitude of events pulling at my attention and time. Often they are of little consequence and I'm able to stifle an outburst. But more serious are the long-term, unremitting problems that build like thunderclouds. I pray I will learn to recognize the growing tension and take action so it will dissipate rather than erupt. Dear Father, prevent me from letting anger manage me.

The Power of a Healthy Lifestyle

Exercise and proper nutrition help keep the body healthy. At one time, the daily struggle to gather food ensured sufficient activity. The Bible says, "By the sweat of your brow you will eat your food" (Genesis 3:19). For most of history, humans labored long hours in the field, gathering crops or hunting for food. Now we live sedentary lives—we don't even slice our own pizza. But we still exercise for good health.

The advantage of a healthy lifestyle is that the extra years of increased life expectancy aren't tacked on at the end of a person's life but inserted in the middle years. A thirty-year-old with a sound body is more likely to keep that vigor well into his sixties, with proper diet and exercise. Activities that promote fitness include running, riding a bicycle, swimming, and walking. Some people wear a pedometer with the goal of taking at least ten thousand steps (about five miles) each day.

Exercise improves the vascular system and strengthens the heart. The heart is a muscular blood pump that is a little larger than the size of a fist. A human heart will beat about three billion times in an average lifetime as it pumps blood throughout the body. Each pound of flesh carries about two hundred miles of blood vessels. The vast number of blood vessels explains why excess weight is so detrimental. The heart must force blood through two hundred miles of capillaries for each pound of fat.

The advantages of a workout for the heart and blood vessels are well publicized. Often overlooked are benefits to the lymphatic system. Elements of blood that seep out of the capillaries are scavenged by the lymph system. Lymph vessels have no pump. Instead, the squeezing action of muscle contractions moves lymph on its journey back to the bloodstream. Without exercise, the liquid would pool and become stagnant.

The second key to good health is proper nutrition. One guide to good food is to remember the ditty "Read the label to set a better table." The three most important numbers on the label are for calories, fat grams, and fiber grams. When weight increases, substitute foods that are lower in calories, lower in fat grams, and higher in fiber grams.

The price of a meal has little bearing on its wholesomeness. Generally, inexpensive foods are just as healthful, or more so, than more expensive ones. However, time is a factor because preparing a good meal usually takes time. Warming up a TV dinner or picking up takeout from a fast-food restaurant may be quick, but the food usually isn't as nourishing as a meal made from scratch with wholesome and tasty ingredients.

A healthy life is linked to a relationship with God: "Do you not know that your body is a temple of the Holy Spirit, who is in you, whom you have received from God? You are not your own; you were bought at a price. Therefore honor God with your body" (1 Corinthians 6:19–20).

Hezekiah's Prayer for Healing

*I*n those days Hezekiah became ill and was at the point of death. . . . Hezekiah. . .prayed to the LORD, "Remember, O LORD, how I have walked before you faithfully and with wholehearted devotion and have done what is good in your eyes." And Hezekiah wept bitterly.

. . . [God told Isaiah,] "Go back and tell Hezekiah, the leader of my people, 'This is what the LORD, the God of your father David, says: I have heard your prayer and seen your tears; I will heal you'" (2 Kings 20:1–3, 5).

Able-Bodied

*L*ord, when I awoke to bad winter weather, I delayed facing the struggle of getting to work. I called in to report that I would be delayed. The receptionist—a paraplegic—took my message. She had managed to be on time. How embarrassing. Lord, I appreciate that I'm able-bodied. Strengthen my will to be as strong as my body to fulfill all of my obligations without excuse.

Sound Mind

*F*ather, when I become frustrated and angry I need to watch how I unburden myself. I must be considerate of my wife, affectionate toward my children, kind to my neighbor, friendly to my coworkers, and deferential to my employer. Father, I pray that when stress becomes too intense to manage, I will come to You. Let me talk it over with You in prayer. Restore to me a sound mind.

View with Alarm

*H*eavenly Father, news broadcasts often view with alarm a new health risk: a deadly virus or disease resistant to all known treatments. Lord, just as each day brings new health risks, each day brings new spiritual risks. Each advance in technology is put to use for evil as quickly as for good. I know, Lord, that the way to avoid new paths to sin is to depend on You. With Your help, I will guard against the rise of new outlets for my darker nature.

Miracle Cure

*L*ord, as medical researchers carry out their roles, they have studied the marvelous complexity of the human body. They have developed drugs to treat a variety of ailments. Some drugs are so effective that they are called wonder drugs. But I also know that some diseases require a miracle cure that only You can provide. I pray that when I'm sick, I will come to You in prayer, never doubting that You can give healing.

Centurion's Request

*T*he centurion replied, "Lord, I do not deserve to have you come under my roof. But just say the word, and my servant will be healed. For I myself am a man under authority, with soldiers under me. I tell this one, 'Go,' and he goes; and that one, 'Come,' and he comes. I say to my servant, 'Do this,' and he does it."

When Jesus heard this, he was astonished and said to those following him, "I tell you the truth, I have not found anyone in Israel with such great faith" (Matthew 8:8–10).

Healthy Lifestyle

*L*ord, I understand the importance of a healthy lifestyle. Eat right, sleep well, exercise regularly, renew myself with recreation, and have a positive outlook. But I realize a healthy spiritual life is of greater importance. I will read the Bible, meditate on Your love, seek the guidance of the Holy Spirit, and accept the grace of Jesus. Teach me to attain a sound body and a sound mind by living in Your will.

Physically Feeble

*F*ather, I need to improve my physical well-being. But knowing what I should do and doing it are two entirely different ideas. Lord, I have studied Your Word and know what I need to do as a Christian. I pray I will listen to the guidance of the Holy Spirit and make the decision to take appropriate action. As with exercise, investment of my time and energy will eventually result in greater rewards that make the effort worthwhile.

Toll of the Ages

*D*ear Lord, what has happened to my razor-sharp mind? I used to keep a dozen tasks in memory at once. Now sticky notes and a to-do list are all that keep me focused. If this goes on, I'll be driving slowly in the fast lane and have my left turn signal on for a hundred miles. Yes, Lord, I'm aging. Rather than letting age be an excuse to relinquish my responsibilities, may I use the wisdom I've gained to be more effective, not less, as age takes it toll.

He Lifted Me

I waited patiently for the LORD; he turned to me and heard my cry. He lifted me out of the slimy pit, out of the mud and mire; he set my feet on a rock and gave me a firm place to stand. He put a new song in my mouth, a hymn of praise to our God. Many will see and fear and put their trust in the LORD (Psalm 40:1–3).

Sickness and Health

*D*ear Father, I know the devil uses my physical condition as a way to break my bond with You. Should I enjoy unbroken health, the devil will whisper that I don't need You. Should I succumb to an illness, the devil will try to make me question Your concern for me. Father, I pray my devotion to You will increase in sickness or in health. I will live a life of faith regardless of my circumstances.

Mortality

*L*ord, as a child, I read biographies of famous people that ended by telling how they died. I'm thankful I have a greater understanding of the reality of mortality because it was integrated into my experience from an early age. Lord, I ask that I not be morbid about the subject but accept my eventual death as merely another stage in my life.

Desolate and Alone

*F*ather, as I began my teen years, an older friend of the family mentioned the turbulent times I would face, but he assured me I would come out on the other side. Often I did feel desolate and alone, but You saw me through. Today when anxiety, inadequacy, or despair troubles my mind, I survive because I know Your strength. I will come out on the other side filled with Your hope, joy, and peace.

Power of Prayer

*I*s any one of you in trouble? He should pray. Is anyone happy? Let him sing songs of praise. Is any one of you sick? He should call the elders of the church to pray over him and anoint him with oil in the name of the Lord. And the prayer offered in faith will make the sick person well; the Lord will raise him up. If he has sinned, he will be forgiven. Therefore confess your sins to each other and pray for each other so that you may be healed. The prayer of a righteous man is powerful and effective (James 5:13–16).

Emotional Warmth

*F*ather, on especially cold days, after our children have played outside, my wife puts blankets in the clothes dryer. When the children come in, she wraps them in the warm blankets. Lord, when troublesome events cause icy fear to grip my heart, I'm thankful for the warmth of prayer and Your Word. They drive away the troubling thoughts and replace them with the restful assurance that I'm wrapped in the warmth of Your love.

Obsessed

*H*eavenly Father, I know obsessive behavior adds to my problems. On some occasions, I've worked so hard to achieve perfection that I accomplished the opposite effect. A finished project with minor flaws is better than a half-done one that is never finished. Becoming obsessed about my health can be counterproductive, too. Counting heartbeats doesn't make the heart stronger, but exercising does. I ask for the wisdom to maintain a healthy body without becoming fanatical about it.

My Joy

The Power of Shared Happiness

Of all the emotions that can be interpreted as a sign of joy—happiness, pleasure, delight, enjoyment—most have a fleeting nature. Joy stands out as the richest and fullest measure of a person's state of mind. It's the most permanent because it's the deepest.

Joy is a measure of maturity. Unlike laughter, joy doesn't well up instantly from a single event. It grows as we learn what is important in life. As we become more mature, we reject fleeting moments of pleasure based on pride, selfishness, or greed. Instead, we gravitate more toward humility, self-sacrifice, and discipline. We begin to understand the differences between earthly pleasures and a joyful life. As we trust Jesus more, our Christian joy deepens.

Joy exists independently of circumstances. For example, after his successful demonstration of the telegraph, Samuel F. B. Morse was subjected to more than six hundred lawsuits testing his patent. Spending twenty-five years testifying at trials across the country doesn't sound like a joyful experience to me. But Morse and his wife viewed the court cases as opportunities. They arrived a few weeks early in the city where the trial was scheduled. They visited hospitals and contributed to worthy causes. They helped begin Sunday schools.

Neither success nor failure dampened the sunny outlook they shared together and with others.

Joy should be shared; a shared joy is a deeper joy. Jesus tells the parables of the lost sheep, lost coin, and lost son in Luke–15:4–32. Each ends with a call for friends and neighbors to rejoice when the lost objects are found. Paul urges the Corinthians to share his joy (2 Corinthians 2:3). We also want to share our joy with others and rejoice at their good news.

Joy attracts people. Some share happiness with all who will listen—the blessings they have received from others, the triumphs of ordinary events, and their positive assessment even of negative trials. Joyful people brighten a room merely by walking into it.

Of course, a person can lose joy. Periods of sadness can enter the lives of even those who fervently love God. For instance, David begins Psalm 22 with one of the bleakest sentences in the Bible: "My God, my God, why have you forsaken me?" Yet David's joy returned, because the very next psalm begins with one of the most beautiful sentiments in the Bible: "The LORD is my shepherd, I shall not be in want."

When I feel my joy ebbing away, I take comfort in the fact that it will return. Prayer is a powerful tool to bring it back. My brain can't hold positive and negative thoughts at the same time. By pondering positive ones, I drive out destructive ones. Prayers, especially those of thanksgiving, restore to me a joyful outlook.

Prayer of Thanksgiving and Joy

*G*ive thanks to the LORD, call on his name; make known among the nations what he has done. Sing to him, sing praise to him; tell of all his wonderful acts. Glory in his holy name; let the hearts of those who seek the LORD rejoice. Look to the LORD and his strength; seek his face always. . . . Splendor and majesty are before him; strength and joy in his dwelling place (1 Chronicles 16:8–11, 27).

Contradiction

*L*ord, I'm amused by oxymorons, phrases of contradictory terms such as "deafening silence" or "jumbo shrimp." The expression "grumpy Christian" should be an oxymoron, too. How can I be grumpy when joy is a priceless gift from You? When I start to feel grumpy, let me choose an attitude of joy. If I walk in Your will, You will guide me to what is best for me. I can be a joyful Christian by choosing to put my trust in You.

Fear and Joy

*L*ord, fear is ugly and joy is beautiful. When fear is vanquished, joy becomes even more beautiful. So many people have a beautiful smile as they decide to follow You. They have replaced fear with the knowledge that they are following the One who sets aside all fear. I pray I will extinguish fear by remembering that I can put my trust in You.

Joyful Journey

*F*ather, I pray I will remember my blessings, not my trials. I want to enjoy happiness and not wallow in distress. Help me understand that happiness isn't increased by material wealth or destroyed by unexpected misfortune. Instead, it grows as I center my heart on Your blessings. Lord, remind me that happiness isn't a destination but the way I make my journey. May my joy flow naturally from knowing that You care about me.

Better World

*L*ord, at the fast-food place, I noticed a young worker cleaning the area. She was working quickly and happily. She surveyed her work and nodded as if pleased with the result. She understood that she was making her tiny corner of the world a better place. Lord, I pray I'll always have the humility to understand that my worth is based not on pay or position, but on whether I make the way better, brighter, or easier for others.

Full Measure of Joy

I am coming to you now, but I say these things while I am still in the world, so that they may have the full measure of my joy within them. I have given them your word and the world has hated them, for they are not of the world any more than I am of the world. My prayer is not that you take them out of the world but that you protect them from the evil one (John 17:13–15).

Erasing the Gloom

*L*ord, help me make joy an integral part of my personality. May I be filled with joy even when I'm in distress for physical or emotional reasons. May I avoid dwelling on the negative aspects of my life that I encounter each day. Instead, help me erase the gloom and replace it with the warm comfort of Your love. Let me turn to You, the source of my joy.

Fond Memories

*L*ord, I have many fond memories. I'm thankful the painful events of the past have faded. Joyful ones continue to linger. Even when I do remember individuals who were hurtful to me, those recollections no longer have a hard edge. I can forgive and even forget dreadful incidents after the passage of time. Lord, I realize it would have been better to forgive more quickly. Teach me to put hostility behind me promptly. Let me move on to more important aspects of my life.

Joyful Viewpoint

*F*ather, as evening approached, the landscape had become bleak and desolate. We'd driven through a valley that was deep in shadow. But we topped the ridge and stopped at a lookout. The setting sun gave us a view of gold-tinged beauty. The point of view made all the difference. When I'm in sorrow, I can see joy, provided I allow You to illuminate my life. Lord, keep me walking in the joy of Your light.

Sharing Joy

*L*ord Jesus, some days I feel joy so strongly that I need to share it with others. On those occasions, I realize something of how You must feel, because You have an abundance of joy to share with Your people. All we have to do is open ourselves to receive it. May I accept that mutual joy and find ways to share it freely with family, friends, and even strangers I meet on the street.

Joy without Bounds

*L*ord, I can easily love my wife, children, and family. I can be friendly to my neighbors and coworkers. I can wish the best for strangers I pass on the street. But loving those who appear hostile to me is a difficult task. But once I pray for people, I become invested in their success. Their being blessed becomes a reason for me to rejoice. Lord, make joy my goal not only for myself, but for others, as well.

Jesus' Prayer of Joy

*A*t that time Jesus, full of joy through the Holy Spirit, said, "I praise you, Father, Lord of heaven and earth, because you have hidden these things from the wise and learned, and revealed them to little children. Yes, Father, for this was your good pleasure. . . ."

Then he turned to his disciples and said privately, "Blessed are the eyes that see what you see" (Luke 10:21, 23).

Everlasting Joy

Lord, You have given me many reasons to be happy and even greater reasons to be joyful. Each day, I can laugh for a few minutes and smile for a few hours, but I can be joyful all day. Joy is a deep, long-lasting emotion I can be filled with regardless of the circumstances. Thank You, Lord, for making it easy for me to be a joyful Christian.

Joy for Today

Jesus, You have said not to worry about tomorrow, because each day has enough trouble of its own. I do face burdens and cares. Help me ignore unreasonable fears that make me anxious about the future. Instead, renew in me the joys You have for me today. You are a loving Savior ready to hear my requests and be present when I'm in need.

Reviewing Blessings

*L*ord, my greatest happiness comes when I'm fully centered in Your will. Then I see all of the good things in my life. In moments of quiet meditation, I review the blessings that are mine: I live in my home with a loving family; I enjoy the warm fellowship of other Christians; and I work at a challenging job. You have been good to me. Remind me to reflect often on my happiness and exhibit the infectious joy of a true Christian.

Seasonal Joy

*L*ord, although I must rake leaves, I can also enjoy fall colors. Although I must shovel snow, I can also watch happy children build a snowman. Although I must race to my car through a spring downpour, I can also enjoy colorful spring flowers. Although I swelter in summer heat, I can also enjoy the longer days outside with my children. Lord, help me experience joy throughout the year.

My Peace

The Power of God's Serenity

Among nations, peace means the absence of war. Within a nation, peace is the presence of law and order. Peace among individuals is the lack of quarrels and disputes. Within an individual, it is inner contentment and serenity. Of all the types of peace, the one we can influence the most is our inner peace. It can be achieved because it comes from Jesus. He said, "Peace I leave with you; my peace I give you. I do not give to you as the world gives. Do not let your hearts be troubled and do not be afraid" (John 14:27).

When we don't have peace, it's because we look for it in the wrong places. Rather than following Jesus' guidance for serenity, we look to the world. Our secular society, mass media, and competitive culture aggravate the quest for inner peace. Each day news media effectively increase levels of stress by presenting the latest news in the most verbally and visually confrontational ways possible. Talk shows invite experts to discuss what is wrong with us and what we must do to improve. Commercials insist that we can be truly happy only by possessing certain products. Listening to these sources leaves us feeling that we are not doing all we can to have abundant lives.

Life is always in motion. New problems, frustrations, and

temptations arise. The small annoyances of daily life cause us to lose sight of the fact that personal serenity is possible. We are so thoroughly immersed in an uproar, we scarcely can comprehend anything different. But the desire for peace is never completely extinguished.

We can't control what goes on around us. But we can have better control over what goes on within us. The opposite of peace is stress and agitation. Whatever reduces those negative aspects will allow the positive ones to rebound. With quiet time for daily prayer, Bible reading, and reflection on godly principles, we can anchor ourselves in something more substantial than what the world provides.

I seek solitude in a place that gives my soul room to soar. In a quiet and solemn atmosphere, prayer touches my heart more deeply and I communicate with God more exactly. I think back and see what a full and interesting life the Lord has provided. I've enjoyed a warm home life. I've been given challenges within my ability to bear. God has been good to me.

Prayer cultivates a condition of calm and peace. True peace is possible only through God the Father and His Son. The Bible says, "Do not be anxious about anything, but in everything, by prayer and petition, with thanksgiving, present your requests to God. And the peace of God, which transcends all understanding, will guard your hearts and your minds in Christ Jesus" (Philippians 4:6–7).

Paul's Request for Prayer

I urge you, brothers, by our Lord Jesus Christ and by the love of the Spirit, to join me in my struggle by praying to God for me. Pray that I may be rescued from the unbelievers in Judea and that my service in Jerusalem may be acceptable to the saints there, so that by God's will I may come to you with joy and together with you be refreshed. The God of peace be with you all. Amen (Romans 15:30–33).

Bridge of Peace

*D*ear Father, I recognize impatience as one of my faults. When faced with problems, I charge ahead with my ill-considered solutions and ignore the advice of friends who counsel patience. Sometimes I rashly act outside Your will because I'm too impatient to accept Your timetable for solving my problems. I ask You to replace my impatience with inner peace. Please build a bridge that connects me to the peace You provide.

Rash Actions

*B*lessed Jesus, I have daydreams of ways that I might be happier and gain greater peace. Thankfully, I realize that I don't have the wisdom to direct my own steps to peace. When disenchantment sweeps over me, keep me from making impulsive changes that lead to even more turmoil. Instead, help me put myself in Your hands and experience peace in knowing You as my Savior.

David's Song of Comfort

*T*he LORD is my shepherd, I shall not be in want. He makes me lie down in green pastures, he leads me beside quiet waters, he restores my soul. He guides me in paths of righteousness for his name's sake. Even though I walk through the valley of the shadow of death, I will fear no evil, for you are with me; your rod and your staff, they comfort me (Psalm 23:1–4).

Don't Panic

*L*ord, David walked through the dark valley, but he saw beyond it to the peaceful waters. When pain threatens to overwhelm my body, when financial upheavals unbalance my mind, when pressures of life descend like menacing thunderstorms, guide me to face anxiety with faith rather than fear. You have offered to carry my burdens, so I will release them to You. I will pray and take courage. You will strengthen me to handle adversity.

Hope and Confidence

*H*eavenly Father, I have accepted Your Son. He has given me the freedom to begin a new life. I have the peace of a clear conscience, not because I'm flawless, but because I'm forgiven. Now I can look forward to a new life full of hope and confidence. I can approach You in prayer as Your child. Thank You that when I bring my wants and needs to You, You hear me and answer my concerns.

Strange Land

*L*ord, like Moses, I sometimes think of myself as a stranger in a strange land. I look around at my community and feel disconnected from it. I realize this world is not my home. I shouldn't grow too comfortable in it. Keep me from becoming entangled in worldly affairs that serve no useful purpose. Instead, unite me with You in peace and harmony.

Crowned with Glory

*W*hen I consider your heavens, the work of your fingers, the moon and the stars, which you have set in place, what is man that you are mindful of him, the son of man that you care for him? You made him a little lower than the heavenly beings and crowned him with glory and honor. You made him ruler over the works of your hands; you put everything under his feet (Psalm 8:3–6).

Fortress of Peace

*L*ord, my prayer is not only that I might hear You, but that I might believe what I hear. When I accept the holy Bible and everything it presents, all traces of worry, fear, and mistrust are driven from me. Believing Your promises builds a fortress of peace. I may undergo trials and experience sorrows, but You will never let the world overwhelm me. As I know You better, I come to experience perfect peace.

Merely Pleasant

*L*ord, when my family and I began our vacation, I asked about their expectations for the trip. The children wanted excitement and adventure. I hoped for something new, different, and invigorating. My wife said she looked forward to a pleasant experience. Lord, sometimes I need to recognize that pleasant and peaceful are worthy goals, too. I ask You to open my eyes and heart to accept the everyday joy that is in my life.

Wonderfully Made

*Y*ou know when I sit and when I rise; you perceive my thoughts from afar. You discern my going out and my lying down; you are familiar with all my ways. . . . For you created my inmost being; you knit me together in my mother's womb. I praise you because I am fearfully and wonderfully made; your works are wonderful, I know that full well (Psalm 139:2–3, 13–14).

Sensible Decisions

*L*ord, why do I worry about problems that either have minor impact or are unlikely to occur? When I review those problems I worried about earlier this year, I'm relieved at how quickly they evaporated. They all proved to be fleeting distractions. Each day I face the prospect of making decisions and taking actions that might produce unintended consequences. Rather than getting caught up in the inaction of passive resignation, may I focus on making sensible decisions.

Harmony

Lord, three years ago I followed an Internet users' group that was vibrant and alive with discussions. Members exchanged hundreds of messages. I came back last month and discovered only a handful of exchanges. I traced the decline and found a disturbing trend. Opinions hardened, and as e-mails became more strident, voices of moderation fell away. Only argumentative individuals who insulted one another remained. Lord, I pray that my association with Christians never falls into this distressing pattern. May the voice of harmony triumph over discord.

Prayer of Praise

The LORD lives! Praise be to my Rock! Exalted be God, the Rock, my Savior! He is the God who avenges me, who puts the nations under me, who sets me free from my enemies. You exalted me above my foes; from violent men you rescued me. Therefore I will praise you, O LORD, among the nations; I will sing praises to your name. He gives his king great victories; he shows unfailing kindness to his anointed, to David and his descendants forever" (2 Samuel 22:47–51).

Deep Current

*L*ord, I saw an unusual sight yesterday at the river. A leaf and a small log floated in the water. The leaf was blown by a gusty wind every which way across the surface of the water. But the log stayed its course with the flow of the river current. Lord, I pray I won't be blown about by the capricious and uncertain motives of a secular world, but that I will be carried deep in the current of Your living Word.

Sleep

*L*ord, as I go to bed, my head is buzzing with a thousand unfinished tasks. My mind is thrashing through a hundred ongoing obligations. My fingers twitch at the thought of all the checks I must write to pay bills. Lord, I pray for a full night of peaceful sleep. Give me a deep, restful sleep, with the cares of the daylight hours wiped from my mind. Lord, I settle down in Your arms. I think only of Your calm assurance. Now I sleep. . . .

My Fears

The Power of Trusting God

*F*ear is one of the most prevalent mental states that limits us from reaching our full capability. It takes many forms, from mild uncertainty and doubt to stronger agitation, anxiety, and panic attacks. Regardless of the form, fear restricts our lives.

Jesus recognized our propensity for fear. His admonitions "Fear not" and "Be not afraid" are found throughout the Gospels, especially as He prepared to leave the earth. He told His disciples that they would be provided the Comforter, who would lead them in what they were to say.

Fear makes me hesitate and delay. Rather than confronting my fear, I postpone action that will bring me face-to-face with it. If I can put it off until tomorrow, then maybe I can get out of doing it altogether. Fear causes me to make excuses and have second thoughts. James warns, "A double minded man is unstable in all his ways" (James 1:8 KJV).

Even heroes of faith have been fainthearted. When God spoke to Moses through the burning bush, He instructed Moses to go to Pharaoh and bring the Israelites out of Egypt. Moses made a series of objections to avoid that fearful task. He ended with the final excuse that he wasn't a good speaker: "O Lord, I have never been eloquent, neither in the past nor since you have spoken to your servant. I am slow of speech and tongue" (Exodus 4:10).

Fear conquers reason. For instance, one of the safest ways to travel is by commercial airline. Yet about 20 percent of the population has a real fear of flying. The fear shared by more people than any other is the fear of speaking to a large group. We can easily speak to fifty people one at a time, but not to fifty people all at once, yet the number of people who hear our thoughts is the same.

Caution, rather than fear, is normal. Reasonable vigilance protects us from the dangers that do exist. However, fear becomes abnormal when we are overwhelmed and paralyzed by it.

Each day we must overcome our fears with love and faith. The grandmother with a fear of flying takes the plane anyway to visit her grandchildren. The young man has butterflies in his stomach as he prepares to speak about his Christian beliefs to a large group, but he takes the podium. He may speak with a halting voice and white knuckles, but he gives his address nonetheless.

In his letter to the Romans, Paul writes, "For you did not receive a spirit that makes you a slave again to fear, but you received the Spirit of sonship. And by him we cry, 'Abba, Father'" (Romans 8:15).

Shield of the Lord

O LORD, how many are my foes! How many rise up against me! Many are saying of me, "God will not deliver him." But you are a shield around me, O LORD; you bestow glory on me and lift up my head. To the LORD I cry aloud, and he answers me from his holy hill. I lie down and sleep; I wake again, because the LORD sustains me (Psalm 3:1–5).

Fear and Reluctance

*L*ord, I have many ways of avoiding my fears rather than facing them. Inaction becomes my method of putting myself out of the reach of my fear. At other times, I disguise my fear by pretending I've chosen to do something else instead. Or I'll claim that the action required is beyond my ability. Lord, change my fear from apprehension to assurance. Help me see that the reality is far less frightening than the fear itself.

Whom Do You Fear?

*F*ather God, I can understand anyone fearing Satan. Why would people draw closer to him and put themselves within his grasp? But what I can't understand are those who are afraid of You. You are a just Father and full of love, mercy, grace, and tenderness. Why are they apprehensive that a life in Your love would be more difficult than a life away from You? Help me show them that such fear is needless.

Cry of Despair

*M*y God, my God, why have you forsaken me? Why are you so far from saving me, so far from the words of my groaning? O my God, I cry out by day, but you do not answer, by night, and am not silent. . . . All who see me mock me; they hurl insults, shaking their heads: "He trusts in the LORD; let the LORD rescue him. Let him deliver him, since he delights in him" (Psalm 22:1–2, 7–8).

Irrational Fears

*L*ord, help me dismiss irrational fears. Guide me as I sort through my anxieties. Help me to put aside those events of the past that can't be changed, to ignore those unlikely to occur, and to eliminate those that are out of my control. Give me the emotional soundness to bear those trials that are within my power to influence. Help me to overcome my anxieties—regardless of their nature—in the rational comfort of Your love.

Fog of Fear

*L*ord, fear is like an early morning fog that obscures the highways and causes me to hesitate to begin a trip. And once I falter, inaction increases my reluctance to begin a new venture. But just as the sun dispels fog, so Your light dispels fear of new beginnings. Turn my gloom into a glow of cheerfulness. Give me fortitude to venture into a new territory of service to You.

Light the Way

*L*ord, one of the marvelous photos taken from space shows the United States at night. It's a blaze of light. I'm not afraid of the dark, but I do prefer light for security and safety. Evil people prefer the night. I've heard that it's all right for children to fear the dark, but the greatest tragedy occurs when people fear the light. I pray I always prefer the light of Your Word to the darkness of sin.

Count on Jesus

*L*ord, when I read the verse about You knowing the number of hairs on my head, a friend reminded me that You would not have to count very high. Even so, I understand what the verse means. Sometimes in my bleaker moments, I think I'm struggling alone. Then I recall that verse and know that You not only are with me but know every aspect of my life and are concerned about me. Thank You.

Jesus' Prayer in the Garden

Jesus withdrew about a stone's throw beyond them, knelt down and prayed, "Father, if you are willing, take this cup from me; yet not my will, but yours be done." An angel from heaven appeared to him and strengthened him. And being in anguish, he prayed more earnestly, and his sweat was like drops of blood falling to the ground (Luke 22:41–44).

Agony and Triumph

Lord Jesus, during Your earthly ministry, You were weary, hungry, tempted, scourged, and crucified. When I feel I'm suffering trials, remind me You have been there and withstood the onslaught of evil people. I resolve to accept the challenges of living for You, regardless of the trials I face. Keep me mindful that the distress of crucifixion was followed by the triumph of Your resurrection.

Challenges for Living

*L*ord Jesus, sometimes I come upon a detour that takes me along a narrow, twisting, and rough road. Should I not quickly return to my planned route, I become concerned that I'm on the wrong path entirely. In life's journey, when my plans go awry, I'm quick to think You have deserted me. Lord, when I'm impatient for a resolution, remind me that all things work together for good to those who love You.

Jonah's Prayer in the Great Fish

[Jonah prayed]: "In my distress I called to the LORD, and he answered me. From the depths of the grave I called for help, and you listened to my cry. You hurled me into the deep, into the very heart of the seas, and the currents swirled about me; all your waves and breakers swept over me. . . . But I, with a song of thanksgiving, will sacrifice to you. What I have vowed I will make good. Salvation comes from the LORD" (Jonah 2:2–3, 9).

Piranha Fears

*L*ord, although the piranha fish of the tropics are small, they have voracious appetites and can consume a large animal in minutes. Sometimes I think my problems come as piranhas. Rather than a large, overriding crisis, I'm distracted by a multitude of minor fears. I can't focus on what needs to be done because of many small worriers nibbling away at my mind. Lord, keep me out of the water of fear and help me remember that everything is under Your control.

Time for a Miracle

*L*ord, sometimes I see a bleak situation develop. To my limited sight, nothing good can come of it. Yet I pray about it and take whatever action is within my power. The outcome is surprisingly better than I expected. Perhaps through the lens of stronger Christian faith I could see the future better. But when I can't, I will merely say, "Lord, it's time for a miracle."

Impossible

*F*ather, I've visited a museum dedicated to the efforts of the navy construction battalions known as the Seabees. Their motto, "With willing hearts and skillful hands, the difficult we do at once, the impossible takes a bit longer," reminds me that seemingly impossible situations have a solution. As a Christian, I have the power of prayer. I realize I can work under the principle "With God all things are possible."

David's Lament

*D*o not be far from me, for trouble is near and there is no one to help. . . . Roaring lions tearing their prey open their mouths wide against me. I am poured out like water, and all my bones are out of joint. My heart has turned to wax; it has melted away within me. My strength is dried up like a potsherd, and my tongue sticks to the roof of my mouth; you lay me in the dust of death (Psalm 22:11, 13–15).

My Job

The Power of a Worthy Pursuit

*F*rom the time of Adam's fall, we have been required to earn a living. Adam was told, "By the sweat of your brow you will eat food" (Genesis 3:19). In the New Testament, Paul is even more blunt: "If a man will not work, he shall not eat" (2 Thessalonians 3:10).

In passing, the Bible mentions some of the occupations of Bible characters. David was a shepherd, one of the humblest of jobs. Job and Abraham were herdsmen and became affluent. Peter, Andrew, James, and John were fishermen. Jesus Himself grew up with His skilled tradesman father, Joseph, who was a carpenter. Paul was a tentmaker, as were his friends Priscilla and Aquila.

Because God ordains work, and because He wants us to be happy, we should view work as an enjoyable pursuit. Most of the time I do enjoy my job, and on occasion, I've enjoyed my work so much that I've felt as if it were a pastime with pay. But in any occupation the time comes when we grow weary. Perhaps the work is physically demanding or emotionally exhausting, or we may be under managers who make many unwise decisions. Or perhaps the problem is not with the work itself. The strain of an hour-long commute in heavy traffic can leave us exhausted before the workday even begins.

How can you remain enthusiastic at a thankless job in which you are unseen and unappreciated? If you can't enjoy your job, then you can enjoy what the job allows you to do. Keep a pleasant disposition by thinking about how your salary will give your family an opportunity to do something pleasant together. The proper state of mind changes drudgery into a worthy pursuit. Should you feel truly trapped in a dead-end job, prepare for a career change. But rather than taking an impulsive action, thoughtfully identify what you really want to accomplish and work toward that goal.

Occasionally, we enjoy our work too much, or we chase after what money will bring to us. For many of us, the temptation to spend longer and longer hours at work can become a problem. Exodus 23:12 says, "Six days do your work, but on the seventh day do not work, so that your ox and your donkey may rest and the slave born in your household, and the alien as well, may be refreshed."

A Christian worker should remember to take a break. Unremitting labor will take its toll on the worker. But it will also have a detrimental effect on the family of such a gung-ho personality. While the husband is working overtime, the wife must take on responsibilities beyond her own heavy load. Children who have a part in sports events or school assemblies look in vain for the face of their father in the audience. Their disappointment and the strain on the marriage can't be easily overcome by a larger paycheck.

Winning Respect

*M*ake it your ambition to lead a quiet life, to mind your own business and to work with your hands, just as we told you, so that your daily life may win the respect of outsiders and so that you will not be dependent on anybody (1 Thessalonians 4:11–12).

Valuable Employee

*L*ord, help me become a better worker. I will take the initiative to invest in myself by getting the training that will make me a more valuable employee. Help me anticipate change so I can prepare for it and be ready for the skills that new technology demands. Lord, the line between my work and my personal life is becoming more blurred every day. Guide me as I balance my work and my personal responsibilities.

Truth over Lies

*F*ather, the custodian at work falsely signed that he had checked the fire extinguisher; the new applicant inflated his résumé; the manager counted rejected items as completed ones; the CEO released a quarterly report that won't bear close scrutiny. Lord, why has lying become so prevalent? Father, help me not to contribute to this culture. Give me no option but to choose truth over lies.

Moses' Prayer for Greater Leadership Skill

*M*oses said to the LORD, "You have been telling me, 'Lead these people,' but you have not let me know whom you will send with me. You have said, 'I know you by name and you have found favor with me.' If you are pleased with me, teach me your ways so I may know you and continue to find favor with you. Remember that this nation is your people" (Exodus 33:12–13).

Job Interview

*L*ord, it's time for me to seek advancement. At my job interview, help me make a good impression that correctly portrays what I can accomplish. I pray, Lord, that I will be offered a new job that is challenging and rewarding. But if the position isn't right for me, give me the patience to wait for You to present the right opportunity. Give Your blessing upon me as I seek a job that has Your endorsement.

Dressed for Success

*L*ord, I noticed people reading self-help books that give pointers on how to dress for success. Men are advised to dress conservatively in a dark two-piece business suit, button-down white shirt with tie, and dress shoes and matching belt. Lord, You have given us instructions for how to dress, too. You tell us to put on Your armor—belt of truth, breastplate of righteousness, feet fitted with the gospel, shield of faith, helmet of salvation, sword of the Spirit—to stand against the schemes of the devil.

Daily Chores

*L*ord, my job can become a steady pounding of dreary, mundane tasks. They can seem to have no consequence or importance. Renew my passion for my daily responsibilities. I know You didn't create me to live a life of mediocrity but of excellence. Keep me from settling for second best. May Your presence be with me in the workplace. Let me be happy at my work and what my work can bring to my family.

Jesus Completes His Work

*F*ather, the time has come. Glorify your Son, that your Son may glorify you. For you granted him authority over all people that he might give eternal life to all those you have given him. Now this is eternal life: that they may know you, the only true God, and Jesus Christ, whom you have sent. I have brought you glory on earth by completing the work you gave me to do" (John 17:1–4).

Serving the Public Good

*L*ord, I read about Benjamin Franklin and how he used his printing shop to distribute songbooks and collections of prayers to the American colonies. The English authors of these books couldn't find a publisher in England because the authorities would not approve anything new. Franklin made a profit and at the same time served the public good. Lord, I pray my work will have a dual purpose of supporting my family and serving Christian objectives.

Public Persona

*L*ord, I understand that having a public persona that differs too widely from my private personality can cause stress. When I must bend my principles to meet the conditions of a job, stress is inevitable. Lord, free me from the need to be something I'm not. Lord, I pray my Christian beliefs that are visible at home will shine through, unchanged, at work.

Overextended

*L*ord, I had a friend who overextended himself in an attempt to have it all. Then at a fund-raising dinner, he collapsed. Stress, the killer of men in their middle years, had almost taken its toll. Father, help me give balance to my life. May my drive at work never jeopardize my health, alienate my family, distance my friends, or detract from my service to You.

Swiftly Changing Circumstances

*L*ord, how can life move with such swift changes? One moment I have a good, steady job. Then suddenly my company merges with another. The reorganization leaves me with choices that will cause an upheaval in my family. Should I move, accept a lower-paying position, or find a job elsewhere? I'm left with doubt and indecision. Lord, I pray that no matter the turmoil around me, I will remain steadfast in knowing that You care about me.

Job Loss

*L*ord, the pink slips will go out tomorrow. Should I be one without a job, it will hurt. I pray You will be with me through the dark days. Help me avoid anger and frustration. Help me work through the practical problems of reworking my budget and maintaining health care. May I quickly move on to the next stage of my life. Lord, I have faith that You will open a new door for me.

Everything Comes from God

*W*ealth and honor come from you; you are the ruler of all things. In your hands are strength and power to exalt and give strength to all. Now, our God, we give you thanks, and praise your glorious name.

But who am I, and who are my people, that we should be able to give as generously as this? Everything comes from you, and we have given you only what comes from your hand (1 Chronicles 29:12–14).

My Company

*L*ord, I pray for my place of employment. I want my company to be delighted with me as an employee, and I want to be pleased to be associated with my company. May the services we provide and products we sell be recognized as a positive contribution to our community. Guide my company to have a good reputation with both our suppliers and our customers. May the company prosper based on its creative efforts to offer products with real value.

My Supervisors

*L*ord, I pray for those in the workplace who manage and supervise. I know they must make difficult decisions. I pray they request and wisely evaluate input from all levels of the company. May they correctly balance their obligation to make a profit against the impact to workers and quality of products. I pray they will have a long-range vision to keep the company healthy as the economy changes.

My Finances

The Power of
the Lord's Prosperity

*T*he word *finance* can mean "to manage money." God, our Creator, knows the best way for us to manage our money. By applying biblical principles, Christians can handle money wisely.

The Bible speaks of being wealthy and making money: Jesus compliments good stewards who take what they have been given and add to it (Matthew 25:14–30); but He also warns of the deceitfulness of wealth (Mark 4:19). Some people become obsessed with wealth. They go beyond merely earning a living and providing for themselves and their family.

Chasing after money is a type of fear. Worry about our finances is born of fear that God won't provide. Younger wage earners fear they won't make enough money. As we grow older, we may fear we will lose our savings. Once we become afraid that we won't have enough for ourselves, we hesitate to help others. In His Sermon on the Mount, Jesus tells us that we shouldn't worry about what to eat, drink, or wear. Instead, He encourages us to trust in our heavenly Father to provide. (Read Matthew 6:26–34.) Our security is not in wealth but in our trust in God. He will supply our needs and care for us.

Chasing after money is the pursuit of the wrong master.

Our goal is to manage our money, not have our money manage us. The motto of the United States is "In God we trust." These words are on coins and currency but are seldom displayed anywhere else. Money tempts us very strongly to put our trust in it and to accumulate more. One principle of Christian financial management is to recognize that God, not money, is our master.

Chasing after money leads to discontentment. Contentment and the desire for still more possessions can't live in peace with each other. The Preacher says in Ecclesiastes 5:10, "Whoever loves money never has money enough; whoever loves wealth is never satisfied with his income."

Chasing after money reflects an erroneous notion of the value of money. In modern society money itself has no value of its own. Money in the form of coins and currency is merely a medium of exchange. It moves wealth from one place to another. One of our goals as Christians is to move our wealth from a place where it isn't needed to a place where it will do the most good. This brings up the question of Christian giving.

What can we look at briefly that summarizes Christian giving? Jesus said, "Where your treasure is, there your heart will be also" (Matthew 6:21). Christian giving is a matter of the heart. Once we give ourselves fully to God, our time, money, and talents go into service to Him. Our finances become merely one aspect of our service to the Lord.

He Can Do More Than We Ask

I pray that you, being rooted and established in love, may have power, together with all the saints, to grasp how wide and long and high and deep is the love of Christ. . . .

Now to him who is able to do immeasurably more than all we ask or imagine, according to his power that is at work within us, to him be glory in the church and in Christ Jesus throughout all generations, for ever and ever! Amen (Ephesians 3:17–18, 20–21).

Ocean of Blessing

*F*ather of all, when I think of blessings, I'm reminded of a statement by Isaac Newton concerning his scientific achievements. He said that he was like a child walking along the seashore finding a smooth stone or a pretty shell while the great ocean of truth lay undiscovered before him. Each day I thank You for the many blessings showered upon me. Yet a great wealth remains unseen. Although I'm unaware of the full extent of Your generosity, I pray I will be thankful for all of Your blessings, both seen and unseen.

Tomorrow's Fortune

*D*ear Lord, my Provider, although I'm not wealthy, I'm certainly better off financially than I was earlier in my life. I'm thankful for the support of others who made it possible for me to complete my education and to have an opportunity to earn a better living. I pray I won't look at my bank account to measure my success. Instead, guide me so that I measure wealth by how closely I walk with You and lay up treasures in heaven.

Expressive Giving

*F*ather, I'm not an expressive person. It's difficult for me to say out loud, "Lord, I love You." I want to express my love in every way possible, including verbally. I also understand words alone can't fully communicate love. Actions are required, too. The very essence of love is giving. Lord, I give to You my affection, abilities, and money. They aren't mine. You created them for me.

Rich in Good Deeds

Command those who are rich in this present world not to be arrogant nor to put their hope in wealth, which is so uncertain, but to put their hope in God, who richly provides us with everything for our enjoyment. Command them to do good, to be rich in good deeds, and to be generous and willing to share. In this way they will lay up treasure for themselves as a firm foundation for the coming age, so that they may take hold of the life that is truly life (1 Timothy 6:17–19).

Abundant Heart

Lord, in my early years, I diligently sought knowledge and skill in areas that would lead to profitable employment. I prayed You would help me make money. I expressed pleasure when my work was rewarded. Lord, now I pray You will help me manage money wisely. Teach me to be a good steward. I know I should bring the firstfruits into service for You. Give me a generous heart to rule over my financial blessings.

Courageous Prosperity

*Y*es, Lord, I do long to have prosperity. I would rather have abundance than anxiety about overdue bills. But prosperity isn't a sure cure for worry. Money can't mitigate a child in trouble, a job gone bad, a loved one in failing health, or a relationship in collapse. So I must turn my back on prosperity at any price. Instead, I look to You as the One who makes me prosperous in all aspects of my life.

Greater Responsibilities

*L*ord, I found a photo of myself while in high school. It reminded me that then I was nervous about passing my driver's test; now I'm concerned about car payments. Then I counted my few dollars; now I check my credit rating. Then I was anxious about passing my sports physical; now I budget for medical insurance. Lord, my concerns have grown, as have my responsibilities. I pray You will give me the financial wisdom to budget wisely.

Abraham's Offering

*T*hen Melchizedek king of Salem brought out bread and wine. He was priest of God Most High, and he blessed Abram, saying, "Blessed be Abram by God Most High, Creator of heaven and earth. And blessed be God Most High, who delivered your enemies into your hand." Then Abram gave him a tenth of everything (Genesis 14:18–20).

Trust Fund

*H*eavenly Father, how sad to hear about a trust fund that has been looted by the individual charged with managing the money. I know You have put me in charge of a trust fund. All of my material blessings have been given to me to manage. I pray I will be a wise steward of what You have given me. Keep me mindful of my responsibility so that in the end, I will hear You say, "Well done, good and faithful servant."

More, More!

*F*ather, I'm amused by the answer to the question "Who is more satisfied—a man with ten children or a man with ten million dollars?" The man with ten children is more satisfied because the one with ten million dollars still wants more. Father, that's a telling story, because I've found that money keeps demanding, "More, more!" Lord, as I work to provide for my family, help me silence that voice so I can hear Yours.

Hard Times

*F*ather, despite tough economic situations such as a job loss, most families would survive relatively unscathed until better times were restored. Yet in the interim, I've seen marriages break up, alcoholism or drug abuse take hold, and even depression capture a life. Lord, when difficult times do overtake me, I pray for calm assurance that You will see me through to the other side. I know You will provide for me.

Impulse Buying

*L*ord, the actions of children who enter a toy store surprise me. Cheap and poorly made impulse items on display near the front quickly catch their attention. I must firmly walk them beyond the entrance to the better, longer-lasting toys. Father, perhaps You see me in the same way when I'm entertained by the gaudiness of this world and it distracts me. Please, dear Lord, guide me away from distractions so I can embrace those qualities that are substantial and long lasting.

Depth of Riches

*O*h, the depth of the riches of the wisdom and knowledge of God! How unsearchable his judgments, and his paths beyond tracing out! "Who has known the mind of the Lord? Or who has been his counselor?" "Who has ever given to God, that God should repay him?" For from him and through him and to him are all things. To him be the glory forever! Amen (Romans 11:33–36).

Mirage

*F*ather, while driving on a long road through the desert in the Southwest, I saw water across the road. The mirage seemed so real that I slowed to avoid splashing into it. I've read of thirsty explorers in Africa who threw aside their packs and raced toward water. The false vision lured them away from a route that would have taken them to an oasis. Lord, I realize that wealth can be a deceitful goal. Keep me from chasing the fantasy of wealth.

Overdrawn

*L*ord, when did I fall into this state? My credit cards are almost maxed out. My checking account balance is too low. I'm juggling which bill to pay first. Lord, when did I begin thinking that I had to have all of this stuff? When did I commit to more ongoing expenses than I could manage? Lord, grow in me the determination to avoid needless purchases that merely satisfy passing whims. Let me manage wisely what You have entrusted to me.

The Power of
Christian Fellowship

Ask many people to picture the word *church*, and they'll envision a building with a steeple. To them, a church is a place to conduct a worship service. Yet the church isn't simply a building, nor is a worship service limited to activities inside a structure.

The word *church* isn't found in the Old Testament. Jesus uses the word for the first time in the New Testament. He speaks of the church with a very specific meaning. The church is the body of believers. He uses several examples to describe His relationship to the church. He says He is the vine and His followers are the branches (see John 15). He also refers to the church as His body. These images show how closely believers are joined with Him and with one another. Romans 12:5 says, "So in Christ we who are many form one body, and each member belongs to all the others." Jesus is the head of the church.

The church refers to all of those people worldwide who have accepted Jesus as their Savior. Often, however, the word also means a group of local individuals who meet regularly to worship God. In either case, the church is a body of Christians who are in fellowship with Jesus and with one another.

The first record of a church service is found in Acts 2:42:

"They devoted themselves to the apostles' teaching and to the fellowship, to the breaking of bread and to prayer." God created the church to have an impact on both the believers and their communities. In this assembly we are encouraged to improve our service to the Lord. Singing, praying, studying the Bible, and engaging in other Christian activities are ways to worship God. At the same time, these activities strengthen our faith and refresh us in our determination to lead holy lives.

Sometimes we think of the worship service as requiring our attendance, and we walk away from it believing we've done our duty for the week. But worship extends beyond the weekly assembly. Offering a friendly smile, exercising patience in trying times, and giving an even-tempered reply to harsh words are as much acts of worship as are singing songs and listening to the Gospel.

The assembly of believers takes on additional importance when we think of it as a training ground that prepares us to enter the world and bring Jesus to those who are without Him. The institutions built by humans—governments, schools, businesses, organizations, and societies—attempt to solve the world's problems. But without the application of Christian principles, they have limited success. To the community, the church exemplifies the blessings that come from being in fellowship with Jesus.

To bring light to our neighbors, we need our spirits to be habitually renewed. Regular meetings with other Christians afford the opportunity to experience such renewal. The Bible reinforces the importance of meeting with other believers in Hebrews 10:25: "Let us not give up meeting together, as some are in the habit of doing, but let us encourage one another—and all the more as you see the Day approaching."

Body of Christ

*A*lthough I am less than the least of all God's people, this grace was given me: to preach to the Gentiles the unsearchable riches of Christ, and to make plain to everyone the administration of this mystery, which for ages past was kept hidden in God, who created all things. His intent was that now, through the church, the manifold wisdom of God should be made known to the rulers and authorities in the heavenly realms, according to his eternal purpose which he accomplished in Christ Jesus our Lord (Ephesians 3:8–11).

Love for the Church

*L*ord, I appreciate Your love for the church. You make Yourself known to us through the fellowship of believers. We are the works of Your hands, and our best attributes are a mirror of Your qualities. When we come together, help us reinforce those characteristics that best reveal Your nature. You are our ultimate model, but seeing others reflect Your love strengthens us, as well. I pray I will reflect the light of Your love.

Respect for Others

*L*ord, help me radiate a warm acceptance of fellow Christians. May they delight in meeting with me. Never should they feel that I'm examining their words or actions for hidden motives. Let my attitude show respect for their opinions and their service to You. May others leave my presence feeling that they have become more solid in their walk with You. I would be pleased if they become better people because they have known me.

Image of Christ

*L*ord, help me cultivate a strong bond with other church members. Guide me in developing confidence in them. Help me be reliable so that they, too, have confidence in me. It's vital that we act with one spirit and one purpose. Should we become cold toward one another, assist me in being the first to recognize the peril and to work to restore fellowship before unity is lost. Keep me focused not on myself but on You so that Christian love prevails.

Honor for Leaders

*D*ear Father, a person is honored to be a Christian and doubly honored to be a Christian leader. Blessed is the church that has loyal leaders who honestly seek after the truth. With the encouragement of their followers, they can concentrate on keeping their eyes fixed on You; we become a congregation with one spirit and one purpose. They need my support. They are due my respect. Give me the humility to accept and embrace their leadership.

Christian Fellowship

*F*ather, I enjoy the fellowship of Christians. They believe in me and influence me to do better. In a world of suspicion and ulterior motives, it's a welcome relief to be in the company of those who choose to see me in the best light. They accept the sincerity of my purpose without bias. I'm refreshed in their presence. I pray I will honor Your church by enhancing their strengths rather than dwelling on their weaknesses.

Senseless Criticism

*L*ord, the church must do Your work, yet every action is an opportunity for criticism. I find flaws far too easily. I can argue with others about simple matters. Even successful efforts can be criticized because they are not outstanding enough. Turn me away from expressing disapproval that serves no purpose. Teach me to appreciate what others do. Develop in me the resolve to replace words that lead to disharmony with dialogue that supports unity.

The Church's Prayer for Boldness

*W*hen they heard this, they raised their voices together in prayer to God. "Sovereign Lord," they said, "you made the heaven and the earth and the sea, and everything in them. You spoke by the Holy Spirit through the mouth of your servant, our father David: 'Why do the nations rage and the peoples plot in vain? The kings of the earth take their stand and the rulers gather together against the Lord and against his Anointed One' " (Acts 4:24–26).

Freedom to Worship

*H*eavenly Father, elsewhere in the world today, Christians face danger merely because they believe in You. To assemble as a church requires courage. I'm so blessed to gather with other Christians in freedom. Meeting with others to worship rekindles my spirit. Father, I desire to take the freedom of worshipping You beyond the church meeting place. Help me extend my faith and infuse my everyday life with service to You.

Choosing the Best Course

*L*ord, effective Christian action grows in an atmosphere of encouragement. In our work, many questions arise, such as which programs to support and how best to direct our efforts. I pray Your grace will be with all those in my church. Steer us along the best course between the rocks of hard-line fanaticism and the murky waters of caution. May we work as an agreeable team to bring honor to Your name.

Jesus' Prayer for His Disciples

*T*hey were yours; you gave them to me and they have obeyed your word. Now they know that everything you have given me comes from you. For I gave them the words you gave me and they accepted them. They knew with certainty that I came from you, and they believed that you sent me. I pray for them. I am not praying for the world, but for those you have given me, for they are yours" (John 17:6–9).

Others Help Me

*H*eavenly Father, help me keep my zeal for serving You. I will do my part by walking and talking with You. But when I'm low, bring into my life Christians with the gift of encouragement. Their encouragement will renew me, strengthen me, and put me on the right path. To receive the blessings that You provide through others, I must associate with other believers. Keep me faithful in regular church attendance.

I Help Others

*L*ord, You sacrificed for Your church. I, too, should put others before myself. I often need encouragement and welcome the embrace of fellow Christians. Similarly, help me be sensitive to others who have become dejected. Let me recognize those who are hurting and identify how I can represent You to help mend their spirits. Give me a ready response with the right words, actions, or examples to brighten their day. I pray they leave my presence with their joy increased.

Focus

*F*ather, without You to guide us, we don't act as one. Instead, we are like a covey of quail winging away in all possible directions when disturbed; we encounter a sudden burst of uncoordinated action. Constant agitation keeps us from concentrating on the essential aims of the church. Our energy is dissipated. Lord, help us find common ground, guided by the Holy Spirit. I pray we will always submit our own wills to Yours.

Wide Awake

*F*ather God, many aspects of my life are so routine that I can do them with only slight conscious effort. For my commute to work, I must guard against going on autopilot. Otherwise, an accident could result. More serious are those times when I've let my mind go into suspended animation during worship. Help me be wise enough not to deprive myself of Your presence. Build in me an upright heart that is fully awake to all of the benefits of worshipping You.

Honing My Abilities

*L*ord, I want to use my talents in service to my local congregation. I admire the abilities of those chosen to serve. Often, I compare myself unfavorably with them. Yet I know You have given me unique abilities. It's my duty to identify those special skills, hone them, and put them to use in the work of the church. Lord, with Your help I will give all I have in serving You.

My Ministry

The Power of Serving Others

*A*s Christians, we are called to serve others. Because we are unique individuals, we have distinctive skills. By developing them, we become more effective Christians. In addition, as we have special abilities, others have special needs.

God has a work for you that you alone are best qualified to perform. He gave you skills for a particular type of ministry. So enhance your effectiveness and expand how you use your special abilities.

You may be fortunate enough to be associated with a congregation that assists members in improving proficiency and applying their talents. Sometimes, however, the number of programs is limited. The church outreach follows well-established conventions, duplicating what other churches have done in the past: distributing food, sponsoring clothing drives, delivering gift baskets, visiting the sick, and preparing meals for shut-ins. Should you fail to fit into these established ministries, use your own initiative to develop a ministry that makes best use of your talents.

Your call is to service, but how you serve others isn't specified or limited by what has been done in the past. Church ministries can lag behind changes in technology and social structures. Your ministry may involve a digital camera rather than a gift basket, a rented limousine for elderly Christians rather than a church bus, a day at a theme park for a special-needs child rather than a visit to the hospital.

Begin a new ministry with prayer. If you are sensitive to God's call for the next stage of your life, you will see the opportunities. Eventually, one of these ideas will rise to the point where you no longer think, *I should do this.* Instead, you think, *How will I do this?* As an idea grows stronger, remember the response Isaiah gave when he heard the voice of God: "Here am I. Send me!" (Isaiah 6:8).

Begin a new ministry with planning. Take an honest inventory of your skills and personal attributes. Think about the life skills you have developed at work. How can they be applied to your ministry? Should the match not be perfect, do you have the time and determination to gain the required expertise? The answers will determine whether you need to work individually or with a group. Most ministries today demand a number of skills and abilities. The more people you involve, the better. Young or old, expert or novice, each one can make a contribution.

Begin a new ministry with perseverance. You may need to begin with small steps and develop a pilot program to learn from your mistakes. You shouldn't be surprised by success. If the ministry succeeds dramatically, you will need perseverance to follow it no matter where it leads.

Prayer for Spiritual Wisdom

I have not stopped giving thanks for you, remembering you in my prayers. I keep asking that the God of our Lord Jesus Christ, the glorious Father, may give you the Spirit of wisdom and revelation, so that you may know him better. I pray also that the eyes of your heart may be enlightened in order that you may know the hope to which he has called you, the riches of his glorious inheritance in the saints (Ephesians 1:16–18).

Faithful, Successful

I realize, Father, that my obligation is to be Your servant first. I would rather be faithful than successful, but I pray You will guide me to recognize and enhance the particular talents You have entrusted to me. Through prayer and study, my goal is to find work to do for You that makes best use of those talents. Help me be able to include "faithful servant" as the chief line on my spiritual résumé.

Sincere Servitude

*L*ord, at work I'm at the point where a few individuals are below me on the organizational chart. Some of these new hires feel they need to impress me. They often use flattery that is obviously self-serving. Lord, I pray I will never view my relationship with You as merely an attempt to curry favor. Instead, I want to be sincere in my determination to serve You. May I never view my actions as justifying Your love for me.

Spiritual and Secular

*L*ord Jesus, when I first accepted You as my Savior, I searched for ways to be Your servant. I focused only on those tasks with obvious spiritual significance. Now I understand that I can't place my Christian service in one compartment and my secular duties in another. All aspects of my life—job, family, community, and church—are opportunities to reveal You to others. I dedicate myself to You in all aspects of my life.

Voluntary Service

*L*ord Jesus, I volunteer in Your service and freely give of myself to those who would benefit from my efforts. Make me Your servant. Make me strong when I'm feeble. Use me, Lord, to show You to others. May the work I do, whether clumsy and limited or effective and far-reaching, reveal You. May my efforts influence others to seek the shelter of Your saving grace.

Spreading the Word

*F*inally, brothers, pray for us that the message of the Lord may spread rapidly and be honored, just as it was with you. And pray that we may be delivered from wicked and evil men, for not everyone has faith. But the Lord is faithful, and he will strengthen and protect you from the evil one. We have confidence in the Lord that you are doing and will continue to do the things we command (2 Thessalonians 3:1–4).

Mission Field

*J*esus, teach me, lead me, and send me. I realize the mission field is right outside my front door. My desire is to open the doors of opportunity as I find them in my community. Whether I plant, water, or harvest, my desire is to be a useful servant for You. Show me what needs to be done, and strengthen my resolve to do Your will enthusiastically.

Working Together

*L*ord, I pray the Holy Spirit will lead me in the service You want me to do. As I become a more active Christian, I will have greater contact with other Christians. We may not have exactly the same goals or approaches. We may not pursue our tasks with the same intensity. Should we disagree, help me put on the filter of love to work peacefully with others for Your glory.

Abraham's Plea for the Righteous

*A*braham approached him and said: "Will you sweep away the righteous with the wicked? What if there are fifty righteous people in the city? . . ."

The LORD said, "If I find fifty righteous people in the city of Sodom, I will spare the whole place for their sake." . . .

Then [Abraham] said, "May the Lord not be angry, but let me speak just once more. What if only ten can be found there?"

He answered, "For the sake of ten, I will not destroy it" (Genesis 18:23–24, 26, 32).

Code Breakers

*L*ord Jesus, I know *pride* is a dangerous word. I've learned that secret wartime codes were broken because top government officials insisted upon being addressed by their full titles. Code breakers, knowing that intercepted messages from the enemy began with such flattery, had a vital clue to unravel the secret communication. Battles were lost because of vanity. Lord, prop me up when I'm down, but keep me from thinking more highly of myself than I ought.

Hollow Man

*F*ather, I once was spiritually dead, a hollow man, walking a wandering course. I was uncertain of my goals and confused about my destination. But You drew me to You, gave me new life, and filled me with purpose. Now I walk a line drawn straight by the attraction of Your love. I will tell those who are in the valley, as I once was, of Your saving grace.

Jesus' Prayer for Believers

*M*y prayer is not that you take them out of the world but that you protect them from the evil one. They are not of the world, even as I am not of it. Sanctify them by the truth; your word is truth. As you sent me into the world, I have sent them into the world. For them I sanctify myself, that they too may be truly sanctified (John 17:15–19).

False Front

*L*ord, I drove around a resort that was noted for its well-kept grounds and finely appointed interior. But from the back I saw rusted air conditioners, broken windows, overflowing Dumpsters, and abandoned equipment. Lord, You have a view from all directions. You can see all around us and into our hearts. I pray I will present the same faithful appearance regardless of the viewpoint. Keep me from the vanity of a false front that hides a repulsive heart.

Touching Jesus

*L*ord, You tell me that when I serve others, I'm serving You. When I visit the sick, comfort the brokenhearted, help others free themselves from destructive dependencies, or rescue the lost, I'm doing Your work. It brings me closer to You. Lord, guide me to a special need that hasn't been met, and give me the humility to do it as if I were doing it for You.

Model Prayer

*T*his, then, is how you should pray: "Our Father in heaven, hallowed be your name, your kingdom come, your will be done on earth as it is in heaven. Give us today our daily bread. Forgive us our debts, as we also have forgiven our debtors. And lead us not into temptation, but deliver us from the evil one" (Matthew 6:9–13).

Model the Behavior

*L*ord Jesus, thank You for demonstrating how the right example can change human hearts. Thank You for giving me the pattern, which I use whenever I can. Lord, a cafeteria server never seemed to see me or to smile. Each day I said hello and smiled. Eventually, she would brighten as I gave my order, smile, and speak to me. Bless those who work to serve others.

My Friends

The Power of Shared Lives

A friend, according to my father, is someone who will help you move a refrigerator. My son, already wise as a teenager, tells me a friend is someone who will hang out with you even if you have nothing to do. A friend seeks out your company. He stays with you despite the circumstances.

Friendship is a mutual bond. Love can be a one-way street, because you can love someone without your love being returned. In a friendship, however, the feeling is mutual; otherwise, the relationship isn't one of friendship. The natures of friendship and love are different, too. Love is blind. A person deeply in love can't see the faults of the beloved. A friend sees the faults but ignores the minor ones and brings the important issues to your attention without hurting your feelings. The Bible says, "Wounds from a friend can be trusted" (Proverbs 27:6). Trust is one of the strongest tokens of true friendship.

We give friendly greetings to relatives, coworkers, acquaintances, and people we meet in passing. We may hold some of those we know in admiration and respect. Yet friends are special people. We seek them out because we want them to be in our lives. Our friendship is not because we work with them, occupy a place in their family tree, or meet with them because of business or other reasons. The Bible notes the difference between companions and friends with the proverb "A man of many companions may come to ruin, but there is a friend who sticks closer than a brother" (Proverbs 18:24).

Friends are equal. People begin friendships regardless of differences in status, education, wealth, or possessions. Those differences can be positive for the relationship. The Bible says, "Two are better than one, because they have a good return for their work: If one falls down, his friend can help him up. But pity the man who falls and has no one to help him up!" (Ecclesiastes 4:9–10). Friendship can't long endure, however, if one member is always in need of help. Each member must bring something to share with the other.

Friendship takes time and commitment. We can act friendly toward all people, but we can be true friends to only a few. It takes effort and work to build a friendship because friendship is not an emotion—it's an action. Friendship is not maintenance free. Consequently, making new friends takes extra effort so that new friends don't come between existing friendships.

The Bible mentions many friends: David and Jonathan (1 Samuel 20:42), Jesus and Lazarus (John 11:11), Paul and Luke (Colossians 4:14), and John and Gaius (3 John 1:1). Abraham was called a friend of God (James 2:23). Every friend is a gift from God. The most blessed friendships are those between Christians.

Perfect Love

*T*here is no fear in love. But perfect love drives out fear, because fear has to do with punishment. The one who fears is not made perfect in love.

We love because he first loved us. If anyone says, "I love God," yet hates his brother, he is a liar. For anyone who does not love his brother, whom he has seen, cannot love God, whom he has not seen. And he has given us this command: Whoever loves God must also love his brother (1 John 4:18–21).

More Than Mediocrity

*L*ord, I pray for friends who are intelligent and dynamic. May we be comfortable with one another, but not so alike that we settle into mediocrity. May their sharp minds and robust personalities challenge me to be a better person. I know two friends acting together can be more than the sum of each one individually. I pray we will strengthen each other's positive traits. Let us be what You want us to be and more than we think we can be.

Deaf Ear

*L*ord, I'm quick to dismiss a rumor about a friend. Should someone attempt to pass on stories of another's failings, I will find business elsewhere and deprive the gossip of a listener to these tales. I refuse to be rash or hasty in judging my friend. Yet I realize that my actions for a friend should extend to all people, especially Christians. Give me the courtesy to act in love toward all people.

Green-Eyed Monster

*L*ord, I find it easier to grieve at a friend's hardship than to rejoice at his good fortune. I help him and wish him well. But when his success is great, I feel a twinge of regret that I wasn't the one who received the reward. The green-eyed monster of envy is strong in me. Lord, fill my heart with love so that envy is driven out. I ask for a pure heart that rejects envy of my friend and embraces happiness for him.

Perfect Storm

*L*ord, during a perfect ice storm, our subdivision endured five days without electricity. One neighbor had a gas hot water heater, so he invited us to take hot showers at his house. Another neighbor cooked for us on his patio grill. We all got an early start on recovery by clearing away the broken limbs. Sharing our different skills allowed us to minimize the severity of the situation. Lord, thank You for neighbors who pull together in times of adversity.

Standing against the Devil

*F*inally, be strong in the Lord and in his mighty power. Put on the full armor of God so that you can take your stand against the devil's schemes. For our struggle is not against flesh and blood, but against the rulers, against the authorities, against the powers of this dark world and against the spiritual forces of evil in the heavenly realms (Ephesians 6:10–12).

Mutual Influence

*L*ord, I know my choice of friends will profoundly affect my life. I can't walk with You if I'm walking with friends who have no regard for You. I ask You to provide me with the opportunity to develop friendships that will add souls to Your kingdom. May my friends and I have a mutual influence for good. May we see You in one another and come to share a determination to be effective Christians.

Friendly Help

*L*ord, I came upon a motorcycle accident a moment after it happened. As the accident victim righted his motorcycle, he brushed aside all attempts to help, even from his friend. I, too, find myself unwilling to accept the attention of others, even when the offer is from my friends. Pride stands in the way of my consenting to their aid. Lord, forgive my attempts at self-sufficiency. May I humbly accept help from others and from You.

Pool of Friends

*L*ord, some people collect new friends merely by shaking their hands. My pace of making another friend is far less swift. Even as new friendships grow, older ones seem to fade away. I know You express Your love through those around me. I ask You to build in me the characteristics that others find attractive. May I have compassion, trust, acceptance, and optimism for lasting friendships.

Lonely Hearts

*L*ord, he knocked on my door and asked for help with his bookkeeping studies. I knew him only slightly, but we had some interests in common. He hesitantly asked for my help. The question took only a few minutes to answer, but he delayed leaving for an hour or more as we talked. Sometimes I grew impatient with him. Lord, why wasn't I sensitive enough to understand that he was merely lonely and needed human contact? Please, Lord, open my eyes to the needs of others.

Thanksgiving

I always thank my God as I remember you in my prayers, because I hear about your faith in the Lord Jesus and your love for all the saints. I pray that you may be active in sharing your faith, so that you will have a full understanding of every good thing we in Christ. Your love has given me great joy and encouragement, because you, brother, have refreshed the hearts of the saints (Philemon 1:4–7).

Destination

*L*ord, I'm always telling my friends of a great place to fish, a good but inexpensive restaurant, or an interesting vacation destination. Often they take my advice and report on their experience at the same location. Lord, a heavenly home with You is immeasurably more important than a vacation destination. Help me talk to my friends about that destination with the same fervor I use when describing earthly destinations.

Mindful of Friends

*L*ord, a friend bought a book for me at a used bookstore. He had been shopping for himself but thought of me, too. It's difficult for me to have friends in mind when I'm shopping for myself. Lord, You are a faithful friend who is always thinking of ways to bless me. I ask that I, too, will be faithful to You and mindful of my friends.

Greater Love

*M*y command is this: Love each other as I have loved you. Greater love has no one than this, that he lay down his life for his friends. You are my friends if you do what I command. I no longer call you servants, because a servant does not know his master's business. Instead, I have called you friends, for everything that I learned from my Father I have made known to you (John 15:12–15).

Enabler

*L*ord, I'm aware that loyalty and support are two of the most admired traits a person can exhibit. By standing with those I love, I enrich their lives. By encouraging them and cultivating what is best in them, I help them achieve more than they would alone. Lord, help me build healthy relationships in which I become an enabler of others. May I live a life in which I put others first.

One Another

*L*ord, the Bible describes how we are to treat one another: Love one another, be devoted to one another, honor one another, accept one another, serve one another, be compassionate toward one another, and encourage one another. Being a friend takes an investment of time and patience. Lord, help me make this investment without expecting a return. May I not think about what is in it for me but what I can do for others.

My Extended Family

The Power of an Unbroken Circle

*A*n immediate family is usually limited to parents and children. Sometimes grandparents are included, especially if they live in the same house or nearby and help with the child rearing. The Bible says Timothy received Bible instruction from both his mother, Eunice, and his grandmother Lois (2 Timothy 1:5). When the immediate family is limited in size, the extended family becomes more important.

An extended family is made of people related by blood or marriage: aunts, uncles, cousins, and in-laws. Jesus' extended family may have been a large one. At age twelve He became lost from His parents because they believed He was traveling with kinfolk. The Bible names some members of His extended family, including Elizabeth, who was a relative of Mary; her husband, Zechariah; and their son, who would become known as John the Baptist (Luke 1:36–40, 63).

Today, extended families often include nonrelatives. Family size has shrunk, so parents turn to nonrelatives for help with child rearing. A neighbor, coach, or someone who takes a special interest in a child may be invited to family gatherings. The expression "He's just like family" is a common one.

The largest family group of all is the family of God, which includes people we haven't even met. Christians are encouraged to be kind to all people, including strangers. The Bible says, "Do not forget to entertain strangers, for by so doing some people have entertained angels without knowing it" (Hebrews 13:2). Joseph, Mary, and baby Jesus had to depend on the goodwill of strangers when they fled to Egypt to avoid the murderous intent of Herod (Matthew 2:13). The Egyptians who helped Joseph's little family were aiding strangers. In their kindness, they didn't know they were helping Jesus, the Son of God and Savior of the world.

Later, Jesus emphasized the fact that all people are children of God, even members of a hated and despised race. In the parable of the Good Samaritan, Jesus tells of a Samaritan who helped a stranger who had been robbed and beaten. Actually, the word "good" before "Samaritan" isn't used as Christ tells the parable, and using that word alters the actual force of the parable. The Jews of Jesus' day didn't view Samaritans as "good." Instead, Samaritans were considered contemptible heretics with whom no good Jew would associate. With this background, Jesus' story becomes even more meaningful. All people are equal in the sight of God.

Whether a person is a member of my immediate family or my extended family, a neighbor, or a stranger, he is deserving of my consideration, assistance, and prayers.

Noah's Family Is Saved

*T*his is the account of Noah. Noah was a righteous man, blameless among the people of his time, and he walked with God. Noah had three sons: Shem, Ham and Japheth.

Now the earth was corrupt in God's sight and was full of violence. . . .

"But I will establish my covenant with you, and you will enter the ark—you and your sons and your wife and your sons' wives with you" (Genesis 6:9–11, 18).

Family Reunion

*L*ord, when I review the list of attendees at the family reunion, I realize that many are in need of salvation. Sometimes I find that my prayers for salvation for the lost have become routine. I understand the lack of fervor is because my prayers are not from my heart. Help me recognize that souls are precious. Give me a sense of personal responsibility for the unsaved.

Flying in Formation

*L*ord, I read about the Battle of Britain during World War II. German bombers approached with their escort of fighters. British Spitfire pilots developed a strategy for breaking up the formation of enemy aircraft. Separated from one another, the enemy lost their imposing advantage. Lord, I know Satan seeks division. Individually, we are far less effective than when we work together with a common purpose. I pray we will bind ourselves into a wide network that brings others to You.

Future Leaders

*L*ord, I thank You for the young lives in our extended family— sons, daughters, nephews, nieces, and grandchildren. When I look at them, I see future achievements that will eclipse anything I have done. I ask that You direct their energies. May we ground them in Your Word and encourage them to seek Your guidance in their lives. Help them grow into the Christian leaders You want them to be.

Salvation for All

I was in the city of Joppa praying, and in a trance I saw a vision. I saw something like a large sheet being let down from heaven by its four corners, and it came down to where I was. I looked into it and saw four-footed animals of the earth, wild beasts, reptiles, and birds of the air. Then I heard a voice telling me, "Get up, Peter. Kill and eat."

I replied, "Surely not, Lord! Nothing impure or unclean has ever entered my mouth."

The voice spoke from heaven a second time, "Do not call anything impure that God has made clean" (Acts 11:5–9).

Heart Inspector

*L*ord, guide me in being an ambassador of Your kingdom to those I meet. When someone asks for help, I can't see the content of his heart. I don't always know his motivation. Instill in me the resolve to speak in love and raise my hands in assistance. Bless, protect, and guide me in my service to others. May I hasten to help them as You come to answer the pleas of those in need.

Get It Done

*H*eavenly Father, those who give aid to others emphasize the importance of commitment: Once we begin a project to help another person, we must see it through to the end. Father, I want to be a more compassionate person. Give me the ability to detect distress in others. Strengthen my resolve to relieve their burdens. After I begin to aid another person, remind me to continue my support until the job is finished.

Jesus' Prayer for All Believers

*M*ay [they] be one, Father, just as you are in me and I am in you. May they also be in us so that the world may believe that you have sent me. I have given them the glory that you gave me, that they may be one as we are one: I in them and you in me. May they be brought to complete unity to let the world know that you sent me and have loved them even as you have loved me" (John 17:21–23).

Lost Souls

*L*ord, I see signs posted on high-line poles pleading for the return of a lost cat or lost dog. I wonder how the animal became lost. Did it merely stray away? Did something distract it and lead it too far from home? Or did the call of the wild lure the animal from a safe environment? How much more incomprehensible is the occasion of a Christian who goes missing from the fellowship of believers. Lord, give me the insight to recognize those in peril and help restore them to You.

Attentive and Active

*L*ord, in the realm of serving others, help me push beyond the mundane and into the domain of active service. Give me an awareness of the suffering of others. Let me back up my compassion with a desire to relieve their burdens. Often I'm unable to think what my course of action should be. Let me develop a concern for others that is attentive, active, and appropriate. Give me the resolve to do what is in my heart to do.

Jacob's Prayer for Mercy

*T*hen Jacob prayed, "O God of my father Abraham, God of my father Isaac, O LORD, who said to me, 'Go back to your country and your relatives, and I will make you prosper,' . . . save me, I pray, from the hand of my brother Esau, for I am afraid he will come and attack me, and also the mothers with their children. But you have said, 'I will surely make you prosper and will make your descendants like the sand of the sea, which cannot be counted' " (Genesis 32:9, 11–12).

A Reputation to Uphold

*J*esus, to people who know nothing about You, I'm the only example of You that they may see. They judge You by what they observe in me. I must preach the Gospel not only with my words, but by the way I live my life. Help me be a worthy example of Your love. You have entrusted Your reputation to me. Let me fully uphold what You have delegated to me.

Time Enough

*L*ord, I read of an experiment in which people passed by a coughing victim slumped in a doorway. Most of the people in the greatest hurry passed by without offering assistance. Yet some did stop. I pray, Lord, that I will structure my life with time enough to offer a helping hand to those who need it. I ask for determination to put my ability into action and the wisdom to recognize those occasions when I need to do so.

Worthy of Imitation

*L*ord, suppose I looked back and saw a large number of people watching my every move and emulating it perfectly. How astonished I would be. Yet when I consider those I meet each day, I realize that to a certain extent that is what they do. People do watch me. They evaluate what they observe and incorporate it into their lives. Lord, I ask for Your guidance to keep my actions worthy of imitation.

Formidable Personalities

*L*ord, although my friend saw many birds with brilliant plumage in Costa Rica, the country selected an ordinary gray thrush as its national bird. This bird endeared itself to farmers because it sang at the start of the rainy season, a signal to plant crops. I think of the people who have inspired me. Many formidable personalities grabbed my attention but had no lasting effect. Instead, ordinary individuals set me on the right course without even being aware of their actions. May I, too, be a gentle influence on others.

Cornelius's Answered Prayer

*C*ornelius answered: "Four days ago I was in my house praying at this hour, at three in the afternoon. Suddenly a man in shining clothes stood before me and said, 'Cornelius, God has heard your prayer and remembered your gifts to the poor. . . .' "

Then Peter began to speak: "I now realize how true it is that God does not show favoritism but accepts men from every nation who fear him and do what is right" (Acts 10:30–31, 34–35).

My Nation

The Power of Liberty

*M*y nation, the United States, is unique among countries as the only one with a national motto that mentions God and includes a reference to God on its coins and currency. "In God we trust" reflects how citizens of the country turned to God in times of trouble.

In the War of 1812, Francis Scott Key witnessed the attack on Fort McHenry and wrote a poem about the event. The last line of the poem has the words "For our cause it is just, and this be our motto, 'In God is our trust!'" Key's poem was set to music and became "The Star-Spangled Banner."

"In God we trust" appeared on a coin minted during the Civil War and continued to adorn coins for years afterward. However, the words were not required and had never appeared on paper money. In 1956, during the Cold War, President Eisenhower signed into law a bill that made "In God we trust" the national motto and required that it be printed on paper money, as well.

Belief in God is deeply rooted in the history of the United States. From the beginning, American statesmen sought God's guidance. The founders of the United States knew that dictators tried to portray themselves as having supreme power. The existence of a higher authority—God—reminded people that nobody was powerful enough to take away the freedom of others. God, and not government, was the source of freedom.

Thomas Jefferson said, "God who gave us life gave us liberty. Can the liberties of a nation be secure when we have removed a conviction that these liberties are the gift of God?"

As a citizen of the United States, I am a patriot. I will support and defend my country. In times of distress when freedoms are threatened, I will pray for my country. The Bible says, "If my people, who are called by my name, will humble themselves and pray and seek my face and turn from their wicked ways, then will I hear from heaven and will forgive their sin and will heal their land" (2 Chronicles 7:14).

Washington, Jefferson, Adams, and others realized that the Constitution and laws could go only so far in making a great nation. John Adams said, "Our Constitution was designed only for a moral and religious people." Abraham Lincoln said, "But for [the Bible] we could not know right from wrong. All things most desirable for man's welfare . . . are to be found portrayed in it."

How do I know my nation is approved of God? One simple test was written by the apostle Peter, who told Christians to submit "unto governors, as unto them that are sent by him for the punishment of evildoers, and for the praise of them that do well" (1 Peter 2:14 KJV). If a nation punishes evil, rewards good, and protects the weak rather than taking advantage of them, then it is on its way to being approved of God.

Ezra's Prayer for the Nation's Sin

*E*zra prayed: "O my God, I am too ashamed and disgraced to lift up my face to you, my God, because our sins are higher than our heads and our guilt has reached to the heavens. . . .

"But now, for a brief moment, the LORD our God has been gracious in leaving us a remnant and giving us a firm place in his sanctuary, and so our God gives light to our eyes and a little relief in our bondage" (Ezra 9:6, 8).

Proper Remedy

*L*ord, when I review the disruptive world events of the past, I see that many of the problems occurred as people tried to find a social solution to a nation's ills. The experiments of Marxism, Nazism, and Fascism led to wars, racism, poverty, censorship, and terror. May we as people of this nation always remember where our priorities should lie. As we try to solve problems, may we remember that without the remedy of Your Word, it is impossible to have true peace, joy, love, and safety.

Prayer for the President

*H*eavenly Father, the president is the most prominent leader of our nation. He sets the tone for the rest of government. He is charged with protecting our country from its enemies, both from outside and from within. A country can fail as quickly from internal corruption as from external armies. I pray we always elect a president with integrity, morality, and the ability to guide our great nation in the way You would have us go.

Prayer for Lawmakers

*L*ord, I pray for my nation's lawmakers. Develop in them the wisdom not to enact laws that dictate when, where, and how we should worship and serve You. Guide us to make informed decisions when we vote. Help us choose lawmakers who have a deep understanding of the religious foundations of our country. May they write laws that will allow all citizens—as Micah of the Old Testament writes—to do justly, love mercy, and walk humbly with You.

Prayer for Judges

*L*ord, I read in the Bible of those heroes of faith who served You as judges of Israel: Barak, Gideon, and Deborah. I pray You will provide my nation with individuals who have the same strength of character to serve as our judges. Raise up judges who will allow Your spiritual influence to extend into all aspects of our society. May they understand that the laws of our land protect our right to worship You.

Prayer for Elected Officials

*L*ord, I know Satan seeks division. He would prefer disunity in all parts of society, including the political process. I know candidates for office who from an early age gave their hearts to You. As adults they have admirably served our community. Yet from political-attack advertisements sponsored by opposing political parties, it would be difficult to recognize their positive contributions. Lord, please bring moderation to the election process. Keep us together as a people who exercise courteous discourse in the election process.

Jehoshaphat's Prayer in a Crisis

*T*hen Jehoshaphat stood up . . . and said: "O LORD, God of our fathers, are you not the God who is in heaven? You rule over all the kingdoms of the nations. Power and might are in your hand, and no one can withstand you. . . . 'If calamity comes upon us, whether the sword of judgment, or plague or famine, we will stand in your presence before this temple that bears your Name and will cry out to you in our distress, and you will hear us and save us'" (2 Chronicles 20:5–6, 9).

Prayer for Parents

*L*ord, I pray for our nation's parents. Instill in all of us the recognition that our children are a gift from You. May we fully accept our responsibilities to nurture children and provide discipline. When correction is required, give us the wisdom to firmly and kindly select the most appropriate method to train our children. I ask that we wrap our authority in love so our children see in us Your attributes.

Basic Education

*L*ord, to be a public school teacher is both an honor and an awesome responsibility. Teachers are expected to have a ready grasp of the subject, motivate children to learn, tailor the lesson for each child, yet be consistent in treating every child fairly. Lord, I pray they will encourage students to develop a desire for a lifetime of learning. May Christian teachers have the boldness to take every opportunity to express the fact that basic education includes ethical behavior developed from Christian beliefs.

Higher Education

*L*ord, I know an educated population is essential for a strong nation and a vigorous economy. I pray that colleges and universities are staffed with educators who are knowledgeable and enthusiastic about their subjects. Also, Lord, I ask that the professors will be role models of integrity, honesty, and fairness. I pray that they are willing to acknowledge the religious foundations of our nation as they train the next generation of leaders.

A Forgiving God

*B*ut they, our forefathers, became arrogant and stiff-necked, and did not obey your commands. They refused to listen and failed to remember the miracles you performed among them. They became stiff-necked and in their rebellion appointed a leader in order to return to their slavery. But you are a forgiving God, gracious and compassionate, slow to anger and abounding in love. Therefore you did not desert them (Nehemiah 9:16–17).

Prayer for Police Officers

*L*ord, Your Word describes a good government as one that rewards the righteous and punishes evildoers. Standing between us and chaos are police officers. Lift up honest individuals who choose patient determination in their work. May they never become discouraged or allow criminals to cast a shadow over their character. Help us as citizens to insist on fair and honest police officers. Keep us from being a catalyst for corruption by asking for special treatment.

Prayer for Medical Workers

*J*esus, I pray for doctors, nurses, paramedics, and other medical workers. May they recognize that the human body carries the image of their Creator. When they care for the sick and dying, may they show gentle concern as if they were caring for You. Guide them as they choose lifesaving remedies and pain-relieving methods. Help them to have compassion and loving hearts. In a world of conflicting motives and laws, help them resolve ethical dilemmas by choosing life.

Prayer for Workers

*L*ord, I pray for the workers who keep our nation strong. Their dependable, efficient service has given our nation an exceptionally productive economy. I pray that wage earners are able to balance the requirements of their jobs against the obligations of their family lives. I pray especially for those who toil with little recognition and at minimum pay. May they not become discouraged. Give them the opportunity to rise above their circumstances.

He Knows Our Hearts

*F*orgive, and deal with each man according to all he does, since you know his heart (for you alone know the hearts of men), so that they will fear you and walk in your ways all the time they live in the land you gave our fathers.

As for the foreigner . . . when he comes and prays toward this temple, then hear from heaven, your dwelling place, and do whatever the foreigner asks of you (2 Chronicles 6:30–33).

Responsible Citizens

*L*ord, I've seen instances in which national, state, and local governments failed to provide essential services. Mismanagement, miscommunication, and delayed response can all aggravate a grave situation. But I've also seen individuals who fail to accept their obligations as citizens. Lord, I pray I will be a responsible member of society, but keep me from succumbing to the notion that government, rather than reliance on You, will make my life better.

My Dreams

The Power to Surpass Myself

*W*aking dreams that go beyond daydreams call upon our better nature. We need dreams, goals, and aspirations. Without them, we would feed only our desire for pleasure. Forward-looking dreams create in us a stronger character by encouraging us to be more than we are now and opening a vista to a grander, richer tapestry of life. They cause us to aspire to excellence. Dreams are stirred up in a restless heart, one longing to be more, to do more, and to achieve more.

Some dreams may be impulsive or fanciful. But others are more substantial. We can't shake them from our minds. They bubble to the top and survive even in the full light of day, challenging us to take them seriously.

God created us with the ability to dream. He leads us to think beyond our ordinary, moment-to-moment existence. When dreams take hold of us, we often look beyond what we want to do to what God wants to do through us. Suppressing these dreams means stifling a valuable experience that would give greater meaning to our lives. Should we reject them out of hand, we may ensure that we are all we are ever going to be.

Dreams require prayer. Before acting on them, we must seek the will of God. Difficult dreams are not those that require us to do something, but those that require us to change to succeed at them. For example, it couldn't have been easy for Peter to reject a lifetime of training to fulfill his vision from God to accept gentiles as fellow Christians (Acts 10:34–35). And Paul, then known as Saul and an enemy of those who believed in Jesus, had to take the step of accepting Jesus as his Lord and Savior (Acts 9:17–19).

Dreams are fragile. By their very nature, they are private matters. In their early stages they are incomprehensible to others. If we share dreams in their infancy, others may dismiss them, causing us to lose our vision. A patronizing review of our dreams can paralyze us into inaction. Criticism that our dreams can't be realized can cause us to lose confidence. Expose dreams to criticism only after they are fully protected by prayer and clothed in real-world practicality.

Dreams are dangerous, especially to the dreamer, as Joseph of the Old Testament found when his brothers sold him into slavery because of his dreams. His brothers are not the only ones who have said, "Let's kill the dreamer!" Fulfilling dreams requires courage. We may have our motives doubted, our intelligence disparaged, and our state of mind questioned. Or, worse, we may be simply ignored.

Dreams require commitment and endurance. "For the revelation awaits an appointed time; it speaks of the end and will not prove false. Though it linger, wait for it; it will certainly come and will not delay" (Habakkuk 2:3). The worth of a dream is exemplified by the difficulty of realizing it.

God's Marvelous Plans

O LORD, you are my God; I will exalt you and praise your name, for in perfect faithfulness you have done marvelous things, things planned long ago. . . . You have been a refuge for the poor, a refuge for the needy in his distress, a shelter from the storm and a shade from the heat. . . . In that day they will say, "Surely this is our God; we trusted in him, and he saved us. This is the LORD, we trusted in him; let us rejoice and be glad in his salvation" (Isaiah 25:1, 4, 9).

When the Dreamer Wakes

*L*ord, I'm intrigued by the question "When the dreamer wakes, what happens to the dream?" If I have a dream that You have put on my heart, but I put it aside after examining it in the cold light of day, then what happens to that dream? Is it lost forever, or do You impress it upon another person? Father, help me discern the worthy goals You have given especially to me. May I keep them ever before me until they dawn to the full light of day.

Lost Dreams

*L*ord, many people plan on doing something special—someday. Then events occur that keep their dreams unfulfilled. One woman planned for the many tours she and her husband would take after they retired. But he died and now she must travel alone. Lord, I, too, have dreams. Help me focus on worthy objectives and provide me with the time to pursue them.

Chasing Grasshoppers

*L*ord, we have a dog that is obsessed with chasing grasshoppers. He never catches one, and I wonder what he would do if he did. Lord, I often seem to be chasing grasshoppers. No matter what I achieve, success stays out of reach. When I think clearly about what I want to achieve, I realize many of my ambitions aren't right for a Christian. I want to pursue what You would have me achieve rather than what I imagine would bring pleasure, success, and contentment.

Middle-Years Renewal

Lord, it wasn't until a few years ago that I began to realize that time is slipping rapidly through my fingers. If I ever want to do something special with my life, I have to begin now. Lord, help me see that the middle years are a time to grow. Give me confidence to use my skills and the resources You have provided to make a difference in the lives of those I meet.

Popularity

Lord, when I take my child to the playground, I notice that children tend to swarm around equipment based on its popularity with other children. A line forms at the slide while the climbing bars remain unused. The next time, the choice may be reversed. Lord, I sometimes find myself making decisions and setting goals based on what others are doing. I pray I will choose spiritual goals that honor You, regardless of popularity.

Kill the Dreamer

*T*hey saw [Joseph] in the distance, and before he reached them, they plotted to kill him.

"Here comes that dreamer!" they said to each other. "Come now, let's kill him and throw him into one of these cisterns and say that a ferocious animal devoured him. Then we'll see what comes of his dreams" (Genesis 37:18–20).

Dreams, Goals, and Aspirations

*L*ord, dreams, goals, and aspirations are fine if I keep them to myself. But when I share them with others, critics immediately arise to put a damper on my enthusiasm. If I listen to them, they would convince me the best course of action is to do nothing. Lord, with Your guidance, I would rather strive for worthy goals and fall short than limit myself to easily obtainable goals of little significance.

Perfectly Plausible

*L*ord, when I awake in the morning and can remember dreams from the night before, I'm astonished at how incoherent some of them are. Yet in the dream everything seemed perfectly plausible. I wonder, however, if I'm much too logical and much too realistic in my waking hours. Often I have a goal or an aspiration that I dismiss as wildly improbable. Instead, Lord, help me strive to achieve those goals that have Your stamp of approval.

Realistic Goals

*L*ord, help me set realistic goals and not chase after vague, ill-conceived daydreams. Help me focus on attainments that make a difference and choose problems worthy of attack. Guide me in dividing the major objectives into smaller, readily achievable steps. I pray, Lord, that my goals will be in keeping with Your will and that my pursuit of them will strengthen my faith in Your guiding power.

Vital Goals

*L*ord, I've thought about the phenomenon known as the butterfly effect, in which a small, insignificant event has far-reaching consequences that can't be anticipated. What appear to be minor actions do have a way of reaching beyond the present and affecting eternity. Lord, help me set vital goals and recognize when a false step is leading me away from them. Help me steer clear of trivial details that may prevent me from reaching my goals.

Press On

*B*rothers, I do not consider myself yet to have taken hold of it. But one thing I do: Forgetting what is behind and straining toward what is ahead, I press on toward the goal to win the prize for which God has called me heavenward in Christ Jesus (Philippians 3:13–14).

This Is the Moment

*L*ord, I've seen Christians who knew from an early age what their life's work should be. Their path toward it was straight as an arrow. Others, such as myself, are puzzled because we follow a long and winding way. But I have confidence an event will arise that perfectly matches my special abilities. Lord, when my calling is clearly visible, may I pursue it vigorously, never doubting Your purpose for me.

Later Than You Think

*L*ord, I took my father to an old home in the hills of Arkansas, where he'd lived as a child. We found an abandoned building with a sagging roof, vacant windows, and a yard overgrown with weeds. He saw in a sudden flash the passage of forty years. He said, "It's later than I thought." Time can take its toll on me, too, and give me a worn-out body, a dulled mind, or an overgrown soul. Lord, in my service to You, may I never utter the words "Too late."

Middle-Aged

*L*ord, I'm rapidly approaching those years that some people describe as middle-aged crazy. As that time approaches, some of us panic. We think we are all we are ever going to be. We fear we will never realize unfulfilled dreams. Lord, I do have some unsatisfied goals. Even so, let me be happy regardless of my circumstances. Give me the contentment to know that wherever I am is where You want me to be.

Glittering Achievements

*L*ord, I work with portable equipment with mind-blowing capability. Yet when the electrical circuit fails, the dead machine becomes an expensive door prop. You are the giver of dreams. When my aspirations aren't sanctioned by You, they become glittering achievements that are dead inside. Lord, keep me from basing my goals on my own desires. May I purge pride and selfishness when setting the direction of my life.

My Fulfillment

The Power of Accepting God's Plan

*I*n any person's life, the time comes when the question arises that demands an answer: Is this all there is? Even when a man has everything, the feeling persists that he's missing something. "I have a feeling this isn't life, is it?" Without an answer to the question, life has no peace and no purpose. If a man consciously looks away to pretend the question doesn't exist, his life becomes hollow. Only by attending to the question, by accepting that God exists and that He has a plan for us, can we discover fulfillment.

Knowing Christ is the only path to true fulfillment. All others lead to emptiness. By accepting Christ, by living in the will of God, we find satisfaction. The Bible often tells of people who recognized that God had a purpose for them: Paul (2 Timothy 3:10), David (Psalm 138:8), and others. The Bible says, " 'For I know the plans I have for you,' declares the LORD, 'plans to prosper you and not to harm you, plans to give you hope and a future'" (Jeremiah 29:11).

But when I became a Christian, the hollowness didn't entirely go away. I wanted to have a truly significant impact on my family and even the world. However, I thought I was wise enough to know what God intended for me. I pursued my own goals, but that led to emptiness. I recognized I needed to grow, but I focused on myself. The fulfillment was hollow. I needed not to concentrate on myself, but to center myself on God for Him to reveal His purpose for me. Pursuing God's goals leads to fulfillment.

God wants my heart more than any works I might do. To find fulfillment, I first must grow a satisfying relationship with God. Then I can see the difference between serving myself and serving God. When I'm no longer preoccupied with my own fulfillment, I can see more clearly those opportunities that God provides. My fulfillment comes from reaching goals put before me by Jesus rather than goals I set for myself.

Are you seeking fulfillment? Then immediately begin doing what you can with what you have rather than wishing for more. You need not be overly concerned about your current limitations. God said to Israel, "So do not fear, for I am with you; do not be dismayed, for I am your God. I will strengthen you and help you; I will uphold you with my righteous right hand" (Isaiah 41:10).

God offers many opportunities to do good: defending the cause of the weak and fatherless and maintaining the rights of the poor and oppressed (Psalm 82:3), binding up the brokenhearted (Isaiah 61:1), visiting the sick and captive (Matthew 25:39), and bringing salvation to the lost (Matthew 28:19). The grace of Jesus, the love of God, and the guidance of the Holy Spirit will direct you to a special cause that will bring true fulfillment.

Prayer for Fulfillment

*H*ave mercy on me, O God, have mercy on me, for in you my soul takes refuge. I will take refuge in the shadow of your wings until the disaster has passed. I cry out to God Most High, to God, who fulfills his purpose for me. He sends from heaven and saves me, rebuking those who hotly pursue me; God sends his love and his faithfulness (Psalm 57:1–3).

Mission for the Lord

*L*ord, I know You have a work for me. You shine Your light on me and illuminate the path that will lead to my destiny. When I understand my special mission, I pray I will accept it and not stop short. May I seize it with wholehearted determination. Lord, with Your strength, I will follow through to its successful completion. I offer thanksgiving and praise that I can be of service to You.

Emptiness

*L*ord, when I go into an empty room, I turn on the lights. If I must wait in the room for a while, I will pick up something to read or turn on music or the television. I can't long endure darkness or silence. Lord, when I have emptiness in my life, I rush to fill the void. I will come to You in prayer to fill my life with joy, love, kindness, and the other fruits of the Spirit.

Volunteering

*L*ord, You gave Paul the opportunity to mention one of the statements of Jesus that isn't found anywhere in the Gospels: "It is more blessed to give than to receive" (Acts 20:35). When I spend some time in volunteer work, I always end the session feeling better than when I began. Occasionally, I can do the volunteer effort with my family. We are brought closer together through the shared experience. Thank You for giving me the opportunity to serve others and bring fulfillment to us.

Solomon's Prayer for Wisdom

Solomon answered, "You have shown great kindness to your servant, my father David, because he was faithful to you and righteous and upright in heart. You have continued this great kindness to him and have given him a son to sit on his throne this very day.

". . .So give your servant a discerning heart to govern your people and to distinguish between right and wrong. For who is able to govern this great people of yours?" (1 Kings 3:6, 9).

Renewal

Lord Jesus, I'm often in need of renewal. Anxiety, discouragement, and physical and spiritual exhaustion take their toll. I know You prayed for others, but You also prayed for Yourself. I now come before You and humbly ask You to attend to my special needs. Lord, these personal requests benefit only me. Provided they are in Your will, I ask that they be granted.

Capacity

*L*ord, I showed my son a glass filled to the midpoint with water. I asked him what he saw, thinking he would give either the pessimistic answer of half empty or the optimistic answer of half full. Instead, he said the glass was too big for its contents. Lord, I realize my expectations can exceed my capacity. I pray I will understand that fulfillment comes from doing what I can with what I have rather than wishing for more.

Motivation

*L*ord, as my school and college career progressed, I discovered that someone always rose to be better than me in any particular subject. Lord, I'm thankful You don't measure me by the abilities of others. You use me whether I'm at the top of the class or struggling to pass. But I must strive to rise to the ability You have given me. Thank You for measuring my value by my willingness to serve You.

Throne of Honor

*T*hen Hannah prayed and said: "My heart rejoices in the LORD; in the LORD my horn is lifted high. My mouth boasts over my enemies, for I delight in your deliverance.

"...The LORD sends poverty and wealth; he humbles and he exalts. He raises the poor from the dust and lifts the needy from the ash heap; he seats them with princes and has them inherit a throne of honor.

"For the foundations of the earth are the LORD's; upon them he has set the world" (1 Samuel 2:1, 7–8).

Latent Energy

*L*ord, when I studied physics, I learned about latent energy— hidden energy that could be brought out under the right circumstances. As Your special creation, I have the capacity for growth and development. Let me not be concerned about my current limitations. Instead, help me work toward my hidden promise. I ask You to bring out my full potential. I want to be a tool in Your hands to achieve what I'm capable of doing.

Person of Distinction

*L*ord, I know character can't be constructed in a moment. It must be built over a lifetime of making the right choices and taking the correct actions. Help me build my character with the building blocks of honesty, honor, helpfulness, and humility. I pray I will always be mindful of what builds my character and avoid those actions that tarnish it. May I succeed while maintaining my integrity.

Seeing the Future

*L*ord, I earnestly seek a faith determined to please You. You have guided me this far, and I pray I will accept Your plan for my life until I have fulfilled my destiny. I ask that You open my eyes to Your Word as specific guidance for me in particular. I have received daily blessings from You, and I desire to continue in the way that leads to the final blessing of being with You forever.

Glorious Name

*A*nd the Levites. . .said: "Stand up and praise the LORD your God, who is from everlasting to everlasting.

"Blessed be your glorious name, and may it be exalted above all blessing and praise. You alone are the LORD. You made the heavens, even the highest heavens, and all their starry host, the earth and all that is on it, the seas and all that is in them. You give life to everything, and the multitudes of heaven worship you" (Nehemiah 9:5–6).

Best Years

*L*ord, on the street where my parents live, couples whose children are grown occupy most homes. Some of my parents' neighbors live in tight financial conditions. A few have medical conditions that limit their activities. Others are of retirement age but must work part-time jobs. Yet I see that those who have embraced You view these years as the best times of their lives. I'm learning that Your peace is far more wonderful than I can understand.

Top Off

*L*ord, before my family and I leave on a long driving trip, I check the car. In addition to topping off all of the fluid levels, I replenish a small survival kit and check the air pressure in the spare. Lord, my life is a long journey. I need to replenish myself for the journey through prayer and meditation on Your Word. I ask that I complete the journey successfully and be welcomed into heaven, my final destination.

Mold Me

*L*ord, I'm fascinated with unfinished or incomplete works of art: Venus de Milo's missing arms, Gilbert Stuart's unfinished portrait of George Washington, and Beethoven's unfinished Tenth Symphony. Whether by accident, death, or intention, they represent the tension of a work left in limbo. Lord, I know I'm a work in progress, but I ask You to continue to shape me. I know You won't abandon me, and I'm willing to be clay that is molded in Your hands.

My History

The Power of a Forgiven Past

No two people are alike, and no two people have identical accounts of their lives before receiving the salvation of Jesus. Here are some sample cases, reduced to their essentials, that represent the variety. One young man's history followed a straight line. "I was born into a good Christian family. Dad and Mom had a huge influence on me. I accepted Christ at an early age and have walked with Him ever since."

Another man followed a similar path but with a variation. "I came to accept Christ at an early age, but during my teen and young adult years, I strayed away. I became a lukewarm Christian. I discarded my earlier teaching and fell into destructive dependencies on drugs. But through a series of events that I now see were the result of prayers by my Christian friends, I began once again walking with the Lord."

Another man was exposed to religious teaching, but he never fully accepted the Gospel. Later, he met a Christian girlfriend and found her filled with joy and compassion. "I came to see God's endless love and accept Christianity as the path to happiness."

Another example: A thirty-eight-year-old man ignored others' attempts to tell him about Jesus. He lived a hard life, struggled to earn a living, and had brushes with the law. As he neared middle age, his wife was the only bright spot in his life. She stood by him despite his many failings.

But his wife became desperately ill. He and his few family members gathered around her hospital bed. A visiting Christian suggested reading from the Bible. The Bible, open to John 14:1–3, was thrust into his hands. In a halting voice, he read, "Do not let your hearts be troubled. Trust in God; trust also in me. In my Father's house are many rooms; if it were not so, I would have told you. I am going there to prepare a place for you. And if I go and prepare a place for you, I will come back and take you to be with me that you also may be where I am." He never knew that the Bible could bring such comfort. Despite his age, despite his baggage of a life full of sin, he gave himself to Jesus.

Many individual accounts are mirrored by some of the churches that received letters written by the apostle John. "[Ephesus,] you have forsaken your first love. Remember the height from which you have fallen! Repent and do the things you did at first" (Revelation 2:4–5). "So, because you [Laodicea] are lukewarm—neither hot nor cold—I am about to spit you out of my mouth" (Revelation 3:16).

Individuals can't change their past. But they can change their future. Past sins, lost opportunities, and lives lived in darkness are overwhelmed by the light of God's love. Salvation erases past offenses and replaces them with a new life. A Christian's true history begins on the day of salvation.

Prayer for Seven Churches

Grace and peace to you from him who is, and who was, and who is to come, and from the seven spirits before his throne, and from Jesus Christ, who is the faithful witness, the firstborn from the dead, and the ruler of the kings of the earth. To him who loves us and has freed us from our sins by his blood, and has made us to be a kingdom and priests to serve his God and Father—to him be glory and power for ever and ever! Amen (Revelation 1:4–6).

Successful Outcome

Lord, in my past I had a poor opinion of myself. I never felt my best efforts were good enough. If something could be done two different ways, I usually felt I had chosen the way that took longer, looked worse, or cost more. I became cautious about taking on any new endeavor. Lord, I'm thankful You give me the confidence to try difficult assignments. When I rely on You and seek Your help, I will find the route to success.

Daily Training

*L*ord, I often think I deal with one minor predicament after another. But when a major crisis arises, I see that You have been preparing me for it. The little problems were opportunities for growth and prepared me for the major crisis. You are equipping me to succeed despite momentary setbacks. You can see the future and know what I must do to be ready for it. Thank You for strengthening me day by day.

Forgiven and Forgotten

*L*ord, an artist friend had a painting damaged by his daughter. Eventually, he forgave her and repaired the damage. But every time he looked at the painting, he remembered her careless action. He gave away the painting so he could fully forget what she had done. Lord, I know You have forgiven my earlier, careless life. You have cast aside all of my sins and no longer remember them. Thank You for Your forgiveness.

Elijah's Prayer of Self-Pity

*E*lijah replied, "I have been very zealous for the LORD God Almighty. The Israelites have rejected your covenant, broken down your altars, and put your prophets to death with the sword. I am the only one left, and now they are trying to kill me too." . . .

The LORD said to him, ". . . Yet I reserve seven thousand in Israel—all whose knees have not bowed down to Baal and all whose mouths have not kissed him" (1 Kings 19:10, 15, 18).

Do-Over

*L*ord, my wife was explaining to one of our children about repentance and forgiveness. When she asked if he understood, he said, "Yes, it's like a do-over." Lord, I'm thankful You give me the opportunity to start fresh. Once I repent, You erase the errors behind me and give me a clean page on which to write my future.

Success Has Many Fathers

Lord, according to a saying, "Success has many fathers, but failure is an orphan." Looking back, I've been too determined to distance myself from failure. This determination has created adversaries, strained partnerships, and broken friendships. Help me understand that failure is merely a testing ground for maturity. By accepting responsibility for my actions and learning to control them, I'm being built as a stronger Christian. Help me learn and move forward.

Breaking the Cycle

Lord, my early history was one of repeated mistakes leading to the same bleak outcome. I did exactly the same action under identical circumstances and was surprised when I encountered the same unfortunate result. Lord, I know mistakes are part of my life, but I need to break the cycle of repeating them. I'm thankful that because I have accepted You, my mistakes have become lessons leading me to change. Please continue to lead me to a better life.

Sins Confessed

*N*ow therefore, O our God, the great, mighty and awesome God, who keeps his covenant of love, do not let all this hardship seem trifling in your eyes—the hardship that has come upon us, upon our kings and leaders, upon our priests and prophets, upon our fathers and all your people, from the days of the kings of Assyria until today. In all that has happened to us, you have been just; you have acted faithfully, while we did wrong (Nehemiah 9:32–33).

Two Men's Prayers

*T*o some who were confident of their own righteousness and looked down on everybody else, Jesus told this parable: "Two men went up to the temple to pray, one a Pharisee and the other a tax collector. The Pharisee stood up and prayed about himself: 'God, I thank you that I am not like other men—robbers, evildoers, adulterers—or even like this tax collector. I fast twice a week and give a tenth of all I get'" (Luke 18:9–12).

Image of God

*L*ord, while visiting the canyon country of the American Southwest, I've seen how changes are made to solid rock by the ever-present wind and sudden cloudbursts. When I look at these impressive stone monuments, I realize You have been changing my life. Whether those alterations are slow or sudden, gentle or forceful, subtle or obvious, I'm thankful I welcomed You into my life to shape me into the person You want me to be.

Gift Card

*L*ord, You gave me the gift of life. I spent the first part of it without knowing its source. Like a gift card with no dollar limit, I recklessly used the time in selfish pursuits. Happily, before my time expired, I accepted Your saving grace. Now I arise each morning thankful that You have given me another day. I pray I will always be aware that each moment is a precious commodity. May I spend it wisely.

David's Prayer of Repentance

*H*ave mercy on me, O God, according to your unfailing love; according to your great compassion blot out my transgressions. Wash away all my iniquity and cleanse me from my sin. For I know my transgressions, and my sin is always before me. Against you, you only, have I sinned and done what is evil in your sight, so that you are proved right when you speak and justified when you judge (Psalm 51:1–4).

Conversation

*L*ord, sometimes I talk so much that others become weary of my stories. My children tell me they have heard my old jokes and my childhood memories too many times. When I'm lonely, I often talk on and on without saying anything important. Lord, thank You for the avenue of prayer that You provide for me to talk to You. You are never too busy to listen and to hear my prayers.

Around and Around

*L*ord, a pilot friend told me he became weary of repeatedly making takeoffs and landings during his training. But his instructor insisted on being thoroughly satisfied with his flying skills before letting him go solo. Lord, during my early development as a Christian, I sometimes wanted to move on to more important roles. But You trained me in easy, small steps. Thank You for keeping me in check until I developed Christian principles to Your satisfaction.

Spiritually Depleted

*L*ord, I can monitor my car's fuel situation with a fuel computer, a warning light, and a fuel gauge. Lord, during my early days, a multitude of signs warned me that my spiritual life was running on empty. I chose to ignore them for a time and continued on my destructive path. I'm thankful I heeded Your call to make a change. Keep me monitoring my life so I never run on empty again.

My Future

The Power of Seeking Eternity

*B*efore becoming a Christian, I lived a present-day life, concerned mainly with ordinary, everyday affairs without giving much thought to the future. I couldn't understand the ultimate purpose of my existence. Because there appeared to be no answer, I seldom thought about the matter. I looked at eternity out of the corner of my eye and pretended it didn't exist.

I wasn't alone. Rather than being forward thinking, many people who haven't accepted Jesus live only for the present or even focus on the past. They tend to mull over past successes or past grievances and ponder how those events have affected their present circumstances. Thinking of the future would bring them face-to-face with the question of eternity, which they—and I, once—would prefer to avoid.

When I accepted Jesus, eternity became something I sought rather than avoided. I became a forward-thinking person. I became more interested in the future and less interested in squandering my time in vain pursuits. I saw new meaning for my existence. Peter writes, "Praise be to the God and Father of our Lord Jesus Christ! In his great mercy he has given us new birth into a living hope through the resurrection of Jesus Christ from the dead, and into an inheritance that can never perish, spoil or fade—kept in heaven for you" (1 Peter 1:3–4).

My life in Jesus began with a new birth, which gave me a new identity and a new vision that guided me. God lovingly sought a personal, eternal relationship with me. He numbered my days on earth as a time to prepare for eternity with Him. A new birth implied growth. Through prayer and Bible study, a persistent concept grew in my heart of the person God wanted me to be. I allowed God to prepare me for heaven.

Heaven is the eventual destination of Christians. When Jesus ascended into heaven, He went to prepare a place for His people. We are, in fact, already citizens of heaven. The Bible says, "But our citizenship is in heaven. And we eagerly await a Savior from there, the Lord Jesus Christ, who, by the power that enables him to bring everything under his control, will transform our lowly bodies so that they will be like his glorious body" (Philippians 3:20–21). Heaven gives meaning to our lives.

Often the first year after being born again is the most meaningful time for a new Christian. As the fire burns strongly, the new believer's mind seeks with a feverish intensity to become all that God intends him to be. As he grows and develops, he may tend to fall once again into the futile trap of reflecting on his life to see if he has made a difference. But none of us have the skills to judge how effective our lives have been. Paul says, "I planted the seed, Apollos watered it, but God made it grow" (1 Corinthians 3:6). A spiritual vision faces forward. Without undue concern for the past, we look to our future.

From Heaven

*S*o I said: "Do not take me away, O my God, in the midst of my days; your years go on through all generations. In the beginning you laid the foundations of the earth, and the heavens are the work of your hands. They will perish, but you remain; they will all wear out like a garment. Like clothing you will change them and they will be discarded. But you remain the same, and your years will never end. The children of your servants will live in your presence; their descendants will be established before you" (Psalm 102:24–28).

Joy in Heaven

*H*eavenly Father, at the end of the day when I pick up my small child at preschool, he is happy as he plays with a toy. When he sees me, he swoops over to be swung overhead as I pick him up. His face reveals more than happiness. He is joyful because he is in the arms of his father. Lord, how joyful must be the event when we come home to You and You pick us up and we share our joy with each other.

Pure Life

*F*ather, You have given me a recipe for success. When I try to mix secular concepts with biblical principles, the result will be an unacceptable mishmash. Keep me from the naïve belief that I can improve on Your Word. Instead, let me live a pure life based firmly on the Gospel. When my life draws to a close, I want to see a future untainted by false premises.

Brighter Future

*L*ord, because I have followed the light of Your Word, You have carried me through adversity, comforted me in times of distress, and positioned me to receive success. With Your guiding light, my future has always looked brighter than my past. I ask that all aspects of my life reflect Your love to others. No matter what happens, I will remain triumphant because of Your gift of eternal life.

Jesus' Prayer for Believers to Join Him in Heaven

*F*ather, I want those you have given me to be with me where I am, and to see my glory, the glory you have given me because you loved me before the creation of the world.

Righteous Father, though the world does not know you, I know you, and they know that you have sent me. I have made you known to them, and will continue to make you known in order that the love you have for me may be in them and that I myself may be in them (John 17:24–26).

In God We Trust

*L*ord, in my country, "In God we trust" is the national motto. The words appear on all of our coins and paper money. However, the motto can be an empty sentiment, or it can be a guiding principle. Lord, I desire that my trust in You take on real meaning. I want trust in You to be an action word in my life. Even when the future is obscured, I will walk beside You knowing that You are leading me in the right way.

Future Prospects

*H*eavenly Father, with Your blessings I have learned to live and even thrive in this world. Sometimes I become satisfied with my circumstances. Then unexpected misfortune awakens me to the fact that things can go wrong very quickly. Help me always be aware that the earth is not my final destination. The earth is a testing ground to prepare me for eternity with You. Lord, keep my eyes not on my present circumstances but on my future prospects.

Beyond the Event Horizon

*J*esus, I'm fascinated by what physicists describe as the event horizon around a black hole. Gravity becomes so overwhelming that even light can't escape. Physicists don't understand what lies beyond the event horizon. Lord, earlier in my life, the concept of eternal life was beyond comprehension. Although I still don't fully understand what awaits me, I know You have conquered death. Thank You for giving me eternal life with You.

Prayer of Worship in Heaven

*T*he twenty-four elders, who were seated on their thrones before God, fell on their faces and worshiped God, saying: "We give thanks to you, Lord God Almighty, the One who is and who was, because you have taken your great power and have begun to reign" (Revelation 11:16–17).

Future Trust

*G*uiding Father, when walking in nature preserves, I carry a trail guide. It reassures me that I'll reach a destination that may not be readily visible. My spiritual travels are similar. I live in the present but wish to see the eternal. My faith is too frail to see beyond the present. Lord, build my trust to accept what is to come. I put everything in Your hands. Give me the mind to believe the fact that my trust will carry into a future reality.

Heavenly Thanksgiving

*L*ord, each year at Thanksgiving, we have a large family gathering. Each year, I remember with sadness those who have met the end of their mortal life. Still, the number present remains relatively constant. A child is born, a son or daughter takes a spouse, or a relative from a distant city manages to come. Lord, I look forward to an everlasting reunion with You in Your heavenly kingdom.

See and Avoid

*L*ord, numerous accidental collisions on a lake caused the water patrol to launch a "See and be seen" program. When the program failed to reduce boating accidents, the water patrol changed the motto to "See and avoid." Under the first program, strong-willed individuals at the helm assumed the other fellow would change course. Lord, I know seeing and recognizing sin isn't enough. I need to avoid it, as well. Remind me to change course when my direction is leading me toward spiritual disaster.

Praying by the Crystal Sea

I saw what looked like a sea of glass mixed with fire and, standing beside the sea, those who had been victorious over the beast. . . . [They sang] the song of the Lamb: "Great and marvelous are your deeds, Lord God Almighty. Just and true are your ways, King of the ages. Who will not fear you, O Lord, and bring glory to your name? For you alone are holy. All nations will come and worship before you, for your righteous acts have been revealed" (Revelation 15:2–4).

Final Chapter

*L*ord, I read mystery stories and enjoy the suspense of learning "who done it" in the final chapter. But in real life, I don't enjoy suspense. Reading Revelation is special to me. Although I don't understand the entire book, it clearly reveals that a victorious Jesus locks Satan away for all time. I can live my life certain of a glorious resurrection and an eternity in a heavenly home with You.

Vast Unknown

*F*ather, as I put aside my pen to meditate, an insect as small as a pinpoint began to trek across the white page. From his vantage point, the world beyond the edge of the sheet was a vast unknown. It was probably incomprehensible to his bug brain. Lord, I, too, am limited in what I can see and understand. But despite my limitations, I accept Your Word and believe that a better place is waiting for me.

Different World Tomorrow

*H*eavenly Father, my world will be different tomorrow because of the choices I make today. Guide me to the proper decisions that will prepare me for an eternal life with You. Lord, I understand my actions can influence the lives of others and make a different future for them. Help me choose to participate in supplying my resources by setting others on the heavenly way.

Conclusion

The Power of Sincerity and Faith

Power Prayers for Men provides powerful reminders of God's abundance. Consider each of these prayers and how they reflect the challenges and goals in your life. Tailor them to your particular circumstances and adapt them to express your particular needs.

As prayer starters, the prayers average about seventy-five words each. Are they too short to be an actual prayer? How much time should we spend in prayer? The prayer starters in this book average about seventy-five words each. Are they too short to be actual prayers? The model prayer in Matthew 6:9–13, also known as the Lord's Prayer, takes about thirty seconds to repeat aloud. It's shorter than any of the prayers in this book. Jesus offered a much longer prayer on the night he was betrayed. He prayed for Himself, for His immediate followers, and for believers everywhere. This prayer, recorded in John 17:1–26, takes about five minutes to read aloud. In the Old Testament, Moses lay prostrate for forty days and forty nights in prayer (Deuteronomy 9:25–26). As we learn the full extent of God's love and mercy, the length of our prayers becomes less of a concern.

When should we pray? What time of day is best? Morning people are convinced that prayers in the morning are the most effective because the mind is focused, clear, and sharp. Night owls, on the other hand, can't imagine praying with vigor at such a time. They much prefer an hour or so before the day is done.

The Bible doesn't specify a time to pray but instead records prayer at all times during the day and night. Jesus prayed in the early morning: "Very early in the morning, while it was still dark, Jesus got up, left the house and went off to a solitary place, where he prayed" (Mark 1:35). He also prayed all night: "One of those days Jesus went out to a mountainside to pray, and spent the night praying to God" (Luke 6:12). Peter prayed at noon (Acts 10:9). On another occasion, Peter and John went to the temple to pray at three in the afternoon (Acts 3:1). Paul and Silas prayed while in prison around midnight (Acts 16:25). Daniel in the Old Testament prayed three times a day (Daniel 6:10).

The time to pray, then, is anytime. However, God is pleased with firstfruits. Whether you're a morning person or a night person, give God the best your mind has to offer. At the time of the day when you are at your best is the best time to pray. Peter says, "Therefore be clear minded and self-controlled so that you can pray" (1 Peter 4:7). Experiment with prayer time to find the best possible time to focus your energy and mental power to pray about those issues that need God's attention.

Where should we pray? The Bible describes a variety of places where people offered prayers. Jesus prayed in a garden, Gethsemane, near the Mount of Olives (Mark 14:32). While at Philippi, Paul and those with him went outside the city to the river, where they expected to find a place of prayer (Acts 16:13). Paul's friends at Tyre prayed for him on the beach (Acts 21:5). Peter prayed on a housetop (Acts 10:9). Daniel prayed in an upstairs room (Daniel 6:10). Jonah prayed inside a great fish (Jonah 2:1).

Often we fail to pray because we think we must find the perfect place and the perfect time to pray. But prayer can happen anytime—for example, while we're taking a walk, operating a lawn mower, or doing a repetitive task. During the day, we have innumerable occasions lasting from a few seconds to a few minutes when prayer is possible. Some people pray while on the commute to work. Seize any time and place to pray.

However, we recognize the importance of finding quiet time in a private place to pour out our most earnest prayers. The Bible says Jesus often withdrew to lonely places and prayed (Luke 5:16). Choosing an isolated place reduces the chance of external interruptions, but internal interruptions can still be a problem. Often our minds are so filled with the problems of the day that we can't put them aside. Should our prayers be disrupted by stray thoughts about new items to add to our to-do list, then we can keep a pen and paper handy and write down those intruding thoughts. Once on paper, distractions are put out of mind. No longer do they flit around on the periphery of our consciousness while we try to pray.

Take a look at two examples of prayer in the Bible: Acts 12:1–18 is the account of Peter's deliverance from prison, and 2 Kings 20:1–7 talks about Hezekiah's deliverance from illness.

These examples show that we shouldn't obsess over the particulars of our prayers. Prayer is substance, not form. It isn't eloquent speech that is pleasing to God, but rather the content of the heart offering the prayer. God wants the best for us. He will listen to us and answer our prayers when they are offered in sincerity and faith.

If you enjoyed

Power Prayers
for Men

look for these related titles:

Power Prayers for Women
by Jackie M. Johnson
ISBN 978-1-59789-670-2

Power Prayers to Start Your Day
by Donna K. Maltese
ISBN 978-1-59789-859-1

Coming soon...

Power Prayers for Mothers
by Rachel Quillin
ISBN 978-1-59789-998-7

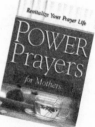

AVAILABLE WHEREVER CHRISTIAN BOOKS ARE SOLD.